Creating an Actively Engaged Classroom

14 Strategies for Student Success

Todd Whitney,
Justin Cooper,
and Terrance M. Scott

CORWIN

A SAGE Publishing Company

FOR INFORMATION:

Corwin

A SAGE Company

2455 Teller Road

Thousand Oaks, California 91320

(800) 233–9936

www.corwin.com

SAGE Publications Ltd.

1 Oliver's Yard

55 City Road

London, EC1Y 1SP

United Kingdom

SAGE Publications India Pvt. Ltd.

B 1/I 1 Mohan Cooperative Industrial Area

Mathura Road, New Delhi 110 044

India

SAGE Publications Asia-Pacific Pte. Ltd.

18 Cross Street #10–10/11/12

China Square Central

Singapore 048423

President: Mike Soules

Associate Vice President and
    Editorial Director: Monica Eckman

Publisher: Jessica Allan

Senior Content Development Editor: Lucas Schleicher

Associate Content Development Editor: Mia Rodriguez

Production Editor: Tori Mirsadjadi

Copy Editor: QuADS Prepress Pvt Ltd

Typesetter: Hurix Digital

Proofreader: Sally Jaskold

Indexer: Integra

Cover Designer: Gail Buschman

Marketing Manager: Olivia Bartlett

ISBN 9781071823583

This book is printed on acid-free paper.

SUSTAINABLE
FORESTRY
INITIATIVE

Certified Chain of Custody
Promoting Sustainable Forestry
www.sfiprogram.org
SFI-01268

21 22 23 24 25 10 9 8 7 6 5 4 3 2 1

Creating an Actively Engaged Classroom

Contents

Visit the companion website at
resources.corwin.com/CreatingAnActivelyEngagedClassroom
for downloadable resources.

About the Authors

Todd Whitney is an assistant professor of special education in the College of Education and Human Development at the University of Louisville. He received his PhD in special education with an emphasis on learning and behavioral disorders from the University of Louisville. His research areas of interest include evidence-based academic and behavioral interventions for students with disabilities and the effective use of evidence-based instructional practices to increase student engagement. He has taught special education methods, assessment, and classroom management courses for almost 10 years across three universities (Kentucky and Tennessee).

Justin Cooper is an associate professor and assistant department chair in the College of Education and Human Development at the University of Louisville. He received his EdD in special education with an emphasis on learning and behavioral disorders from the University of Kentucky. He is a past president of the Council for Children with Behavioral Disorders, a division of the Council for Exceptional Children. He conducts trainings for schools and school districts in the area of effective instruction and behavior management. His research interests include teacher preparation, the effects of teacher behavior on student behavior, effective instructional strategies, functional behavioral assessment, and behavior intervention planning.

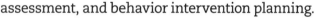

Terrance M. Scott is a senior principal education researcher at the Stanford Research Institute (SRI). Before joining SRI in 2020, he spent 24 years as a professor and researcher in special education. He began his career as a counselor in residential treatment and has worked with students with challenging behaviors across a variety of settings. He received his PhD in Special Education at the

University of Oregon in 1994, and has written over 100 publications, has conducted more than 1,000 presentations and training activities throughout the United States and across the world, and has successfully competed for more than $24 million in external grant funding. His research interests focus on schoolwide prevention systems, the role of instructional variables in managing student behavior, and functional behavior assessment/intervention. He has two other books published with Corwin, *Teaching Behavior: Managing Classroom Behavior With Effective Instruction* and, with Geoff Colvin, *Managing the Cycle of Acting Out Behavior in the Classroom*, second edition.

Introduction

Student Engagement and Teacher Responsibility

Education must enable a man to become more efficient, to achieve with increasing facility the legitimate goals of his life.

—Martin Luther King Jr., 1947

As teachers, we have an incredible opportunity to affect the lives of our students through instruction. Research has clearly demonstrated that teacher quality is associated with increased student outcomes both in school (Stronge, 2013) and throughout life (Chetty et al., 2011). With this power comes great responsibility to use our time with students in a manner that maximizes the probability of student success. Thinking logically, time spent on less effective strategies comes at the expense of more effective strategies and at the expense of probabilities for student success. Thus, it is incumbent on us to consider the instructional strategies and tactics at the core of effective instruction and to make those the core of our definition of teaching.

As Martin Luther King Jr. (1947) so eloquently reminds us from more than 70 years ago, the goal of education is not to create a workforce or to further the goals of society. The role of the teacher is to provide students with the knowledge and skills required to have a happy, healthy, and productive life while maintaining the freedom to think critically and act accordingly. With this goal in mind, research has clearly identified the tenets of effective instruction. First, instruction needs to be explicit. That is, teachers must clearly communicate to students why a concept or skill is important and how it fits into the larger context of their lives and well-being, and provide opportunities for critical discussion. These discussions allow the teacher to clarify misconceptions and allow students to gain both clarity and understanding of the relevance of the content to their own lives. Second, a key component of this discussion is the ability of the student to be engaged as an active learner rather than a passive receptacle for knowledge. But engagement can be considered as both a strategy for enhancing the acquisition of knowledge and a process by which students increasingly apply that knowledge to their own lives.

Third, students must have the opportunity to receive feedback on their performance, and that feedback should be largely positive. Positive feedback builds student confidence and increases the probability of future success. Inability to provide high rates of positive feedback is an index of ineffective instruction. If we consider the first two tenets (explicit and engagement) simply as strategies for maximizing the probabilities for student success, then it becomes obvious that when students are not sufficiently successful, we can consider that instruction has been insufficient and it is the teacher who must change by enhancing or differentiating the explicit and engaging components of instruction.

Inherent in this model of effective instruction is the teacher as an active participant whose job it is to make instruction relevant and engaging for students. Again, we refer to this as a teacher responsibility. Over a long history of educational research, this model of instruction has been repeatedly shown to be the most effective manner of creating student success (Brophy & Good, 1986; Hattie, 2009; Stockard et al., 2018; Teasley, 1996). Because science has clearly demonstrated that effective instruction provides students with their best chances for success, disregarding these strategies represents an abdication of responsibility. The purpose of this book is to highlight the strategies available for engaging students, many of whom have a history of failure resulting in lack of confidence in their ability to be successful, and so do not wish to be engaged. This is important because a student's lack of engagement is associated with higher rates of dropout and school failure (Reschly & Christenson, 2006).

Engagement is a student behavior that is created by the teacher. Clearly, there are students who actively engage themselves in their learning without the need for any teacher actions. While these students are likely not the norm, in any classroom the teacher's behaviors can create increased opportunities for students to be engaged (Christenson et al., 2012). While the term *engagement* can mean many things, we define it as the student's active involvement in a lesson, involving verbal or physical actions that are related to the lesson content and communicated to the teacher or others. While this definition purposefully omits actions such as reading or listening, this does not mean that there is no place for these activities in a lesson.

Engagement

The student's active involvement in a lesson, involving verbal or physical actions that are related to the lesson content and communicated to the teacher or others

Rather, because the focus here is on instruction, engagement is conceived of in terms of teacher behaviors that are meant to keep the student alert and interested through interaction focused on the curriculum. To make this distinction, reading and listening are referred to as *passive engagement*, requiring no effort other than what is often called "being on task."

Active engagement involves students actively using their words, gestures, or other physical actions (drawing, creating, etc.) to interact with the curricular content. During practice, active engagement is built-in, with students actively engaged in doing. But during the introduction and heart of a lesson, there is less inherent opportunity for the student to be actively engaged, so the teacher must provide specific opportunities for the students to respond, or what we call OTR. An OTR is defined as any action by the teacher that provides a curriculum-related opportunity for students to respond in some physical manner (verbalize, gesture, or create). Research has shown that OTRs at a rate of at least three per minute during instruction are associated with significantly higher rates of student active engagement and significantly lower rates of student disruption (Gage et al., 2018; Sutherland et al., 2003). In fact, recent research has identified higher rates of OTR to be associated with lower rates of suspension and that the combination of OTR and positive feedback is associated with an increase in the percentage of students at the proficient and distinguished levels in both reading and mathematics (Scott & Gage, 2020).

The combination of OTR and positive feedback seems logical and obvious. The more opportunities students have to respond, the more opportunities teachers have to provide feedback. Again, if instruction is effective, this provides more opportunities for positive feedback. But this raises an important issue with regard to the purpose of OTR. The purpose is not to assess students, nor is it to challenge them. Clearly, these are legitimate actions as part of a lesson, but the OTR is used for the purpose of *engaging* students. Difficult questions and OTRs that put students in a challenging position will not only be unsuccessful in facilitating student engagement, they also greatly increase the likelihood of student misbehavior. During instruction, OTR is a strategy to be used when other, more naturally engaging activities are not available.

Unfortunately, despite the evidence supporting OTR, research consistently shows that teachers at every level and in every content area provide OTRs at rates far below the recommended rate of three per minute (Scott et al., 2017). When presented with this fact, teachers are often surprised, thinking that they had facilitated much more active engagement than was the reality. This may be a residual effect of the fact that preservice teachers are rarely provided with information regarding the effects of OTR or opportunities to consider and practice different OTR strategies.

TEACHING STUDENTS ABOUT OTR

A large predictor of success in increasing active student engagement is the degree to which the teacher has effectively taught students the components and expected behaviors associated with each individual OTR. This should be delivered in the same manner as has been described as effective instruction herein. Distinct OTR strategies should be introduced individually, giving it a name and a rationale. The name is important so that when the teacher calls out the name, all students immediately know what is coming and what is expected of them. Recall that explicit instruction involves clear descriptions along with a rationale for why and how it fits into the larger picture. In this case the larger picture is students having an active role in the lesson. Depending on the students' age and cognitive abilities, teachers may need to break OTRs down into their component behaviors and teach each component separately. For example, the teacher may need to specifically teach each type of gesture or how to attend to different teacher signals for choral response.

Throughout the explicit instruction, the teacher must engage the students, giving them opportunities to discuss and practice components as a group. Finally, the teacher must provide repetitive opportunities for student practice with immediate feedback before using the strategy in a natural instructional context. As we have previously discussed, the purpose of this instruction is to set students up for success and to provide them with positive feedback. As OTRs are introduced, students need to have enough practice with teacher feedback so that they are confident in their ability to respond correctly the next time they hear the name called.

GENERAL RESPONSE ROUTINES

As we have just discussed, establishing response routines for implementing OTR is critical if your goal is to increase active student engagement in an effective and efficient manner. To maximize the impact, the routines will need to incorporate components of explicit instruction and be implemented with consistency. Although there may be differences between distinct OTR strategies, each will share similarities with the others. In general, it is suggested that each OTR strategy incorporate either an individual or a partner/team response routine.

INDIVIDUAL RESPONSE ROUTINES

Individual response routines start with the teacher asking a question or giving a prompt that has an expected verbal or nonverbal response from either an individual student or a group of students. For it to be considered an OTR, the question or prompt should be related to the curriculum. In other words, asking "What is the capital of Oregon?" would be an OTR if you were reviewing state capitals. However, saying "Have a seat; we are about to start the lesson" would be a direction, not an OTR. Additionally, to be an OTR, the question or prompt must allow for a student response instead of being rhetorical. An example of this would be if a teacher says, "What is the capital of Oregon?" and immediately follows with "Salem, right?"

After the teacher asks the question or gives a prompt, it is then important to allow appropriate wait time. Determining the appropriate wait time is dependent on two things: (1) the question or prompt given and (2) the students' ability to process the information needed to complete the request. For example, you may be able to use a short wait time of three to five seconds before students respond for lower–cognitive demand requests, such as "What is 2×3?" or "Is the word *truck* a subject or a verb?" On the other hand, a longer wait time would be necessary for higher–cognitive demand requests, such as asking students to write down the main idea of a story or summarizing what was just learned.

After the students have had adequate time to formulate a response, a clear and consistent cue for the student(s) to respond is needed. A variety of cues can be used to cue students, including clapping, snapping fingers, dropping hands, or using a verbal cue. When choosing a prompt, it is best to select one that best fits your teaching style and your students' preference. Once selected, it is important to implement it consistently so that the students begin to learn that a response is needed whenever they see the cue.

Finally, the student response will allow for feedback to be given. This feedback will provide students with information to improve or maintain their performance, as well as increase student motivation, engagement, and independence (McLeskey et al., 2017). Although there are many ways by which a teacher can provide feedback, there are specific types of feedback that are most effective. If a student responds with a correct answer, the teacher can provide behavior-specific praise or instructive feedback. On the other hand, the teacher can use corrective feedback for any incorrect responses by providing students with specific information about what they can do differently the next time. Corrective feedback should always be paired with praise for anything that the student did correctly.

PARTNER/TEAM RESPONSE ROUTINES

Although the partner/team response routine is similar to the individual response routine, there are additional components that need to be implemented in an effective and efficient manner. First, the teacher will assign students to partners or teams. Although this can be done in various ways, we suggest purposefully assigning students beforehand instead of letting the students decide. Archer and Hughes (2011) suggest purposefully assigning students so that you can put them in either heterogeneous groups (e.g., low-performing student with middle-performing student) or homogeneous groups (e.g., high-performing student with high-performing student). Conversely, students will most likely pick a friend as a partner, which may or may not be the most appropriate instructional match. To increase efficiency and reduce downtime, you may also consider sitting partners/teams together before the lesson starts and assigning each student within the pairs/team a designation (e.g, 1, 2, 3, 4; A, B, C, D).

After the question or prompt is given, the teacher will cue the students to work together to formulate a response. Although partners/teams can be used in a variety of ways, cueing students to work in pairs/teams may need to involve explicitly teaching and reminding students how to work with their peers. This may include teaching students how to be effective listeners and speakers, instruction on turn taking, and/or instruction on how to provide appropriate feedback. As the students are formulating their response, the teacher will circulate the classroom and provide feedback when needed. After adequate time is given to formulate a response, students will be cued to share it with the other pairs/teams while the teacher provides feedback on their responses.

INDIVIDUAL RESPONSE ROUTINE	PARTNER/TEAM RESPONSE ROUTINE
1. Ask question/give prompt	1. Assign partners/teams
2. Give appropriate wait time	2. Ask question/give prompt
3. Provide response cue	3. Cue students to work together
4. Provide feedback to responses	4. Give appropriate wait time
	5. Circulate and provide feedback
	6. Cue sharing of responses
	7. Provide feedback on responses

RESPONSES TO TYPICAL RESISTANCE TO OTR

As teachers, it's not our job to assess or evaluate what our colleagues do. However, as advocates for the students in our charge, it is our responsibility to speak the truth regarding effective instruction and strategies that provide students with the greatest probabilities for success. When others make illogical or untruthful statements about effective practices, it is incumbent on us to have a logical response. To be clear, we are not advocating for arguing or shaming, as it's unlikely we will change anyone's behavior in this manner. The goal is simply to provide a counterpoint for others to hear and a basic logic to challenge illogical statements. Below are some typical statements we have heard made with regard to OTR and some possibilities for logical responses.

"USING OTR IS TOO TIME-CONSUMING— ESPECIALLY AT THREE PER MINUTE"

As will be demonstrated throughout the book, the teacher can present OTRs in a variety of ways that are very simple, with quick student responses. But it is important to make clear that engagement is not done *in addition to* instruction; it is an inherent part of instruction. As such, OTRs should be planned as part of the lesson and provided to maintain students' active engagement. Because we know that actively engaged students have better academic and behavioral outcomes, there is an inherent illogic to thinking that OTRs take up too much of the lesson. More accurately, OTRs *are* the lesson. Furthermore, OTRs are not needed throughout the lesson, only during the parts where more authentic practice is not yet available. Similarly, three per minute is an average, and it is not necessary to provide three during every minute of instruction. Some minutes may be stacked with an array of several quick OTRs, while others may have a single peer discussion opportunity. It is the teacher's job to design instruction in a manner that best makes use of OTRs to maintain student engagement throughout the course of the lesson. And just to be clear, the provision of OTRs becomes more second nature to teachers with repeated use and experience. With some practice the process simply becomes part of your natural teaching.

"IT IS NOT MY RESPONSIBILITY TO MAKE SURE THAT STUDENTS PAY ATTENTION AS LONG AS THEY ARE NOT DISRUPTIVE"

This one presents a bit more of a challenge because it gets to the heart of how teachers see their own professional responsibilities. We are careful here not to make this personal while providing a logical rebuttal. First, when responding to such statements, it is best to use "I feel" statements that simply express a perspective rather than challenge another person's beliefs—for example,

> I feel like I have a lot of students who won't engage unless I do something to engage them. And because I have that ability, it feels to me like I should use it to increase my students' chances for success.

It's hard to argue against this simple statement of personal perspective. Remember, these responses are not necessarily meant to change this person's mind. Rather, this response provides a different perspective that is logical and nonthreatening for others to hear and consider.

"MY STUDENTS GET OUT OF CONTROL OR MAKE RUDE RESPONSES WHEN I GIVE THEM OPPORTUNITIES TO SPEAK"

This statement is akin to saying that engaged students are more disruptive than sleeping students and encouraging sleeping thus makes sense. To the extent that the potential for misbehavior is higher when students are engaged, we must consider how to effectively select and use OTRs in consideration of student and classroom challenges. Clearly, some strategies make more sense under only specific classroom circumstances, and the teacher must be thoughtful in planning for the most appropriate OTR strategies. But there is also an inherent illogic in considering disengaged students to be behaving appropriately. In fact, we know that students who are bored or disconnected from instruction are more likely to engage in misbehaviors to distract from the lesson or to attempt to escape. If our goal is to have students engaged as a means of maximizing their success, then it becomes our responsibility to develop that engagement.

"MY STUDENTS ARE ENGAGED ON THEIR OWN—I DO NOT NEED TO FIND WAYS TO ENGAGE THEM"

First, if this statement is true, then it truly represents an outlier as this is not the case in a typical classroom. But logically, how can students be actively engaged while the teacher is introducing, demonstrating, and delivering a lesson? Likely what this person is saying is that students sit quietly and are not off task. But remember, we are looking for active engagement during instruction as well as during practice. The OTR strategies we discuss in this book will keep students actively engaged through the parts of instruction that are typically filled with only passive engagement. Even in the most ideal classroom, there are a range of students and a range of competing stimuli to attract attention away from instruction. In this case one might consider the use of OTR as a prevention strategy—keeping student attention through active engagement and lessening the likelihood of the attentional drift to which we all are susceptible.

CONCLUSIONS

This book is designed to provide teachers with a range of very specific strategies for actively engaging students during instruction. Recent events have caused most educators to adjust their delivery of instruction to virtual formats for all or part of the time. This has brought with it new challenges in engaging students during virtual instruction. Educators have indicated that virtual instruction has led to fewer students attending to instruction, fewer students asking questions during lessons, and students who, even though attending a virtual class, are obviously doing other things during instruction—like using their phones or other devices. Several strategies discussed in this book can be used in both virtual and face-to-face classroom environments with ease and efficiency. For these strategies a description for both in-person classroom and virtual instruction will be provided.

Across all strategies it is assumed that OTRs are used as a means of engaging students during the introduction and heart of instruction and not as a means of assessment. However, each OTR does provide the teacher with an opportunity for feedback and some information about the degree to which students are understanding the skills and concepts being discussed. Ideas for differentiating these strategies for individuals with unique abilities are included, along with special considerations for when it may or may not be especially useful. Teaching students about OTR also involves establishing routines that incorporate components of effective instruction and implementing these routines with consistency. Although there are differences between distinct OTR strategies, each will incorporate either an individual response routine or a partner/team response routine. Table 1 summarizes each of the strategies in terms of recommendations under a variety of circumstances.

TABLE 1 ● Recommended Uses for the Strategies Discussed in the Book

STRATEGY	FACE-TO-FACE	VIRTUAL	INDIVIDUAL	PARTNER/TEAMS	QUICK/SHORT RESPONSES	IN-DEPTH DISCUSSION	PREPARATION OF MATERIALS
Whip around	*	*	*		*		
Quick poll	*	*	*		*		
Choral responding	*	*	*		*		
Individual questioning	*	*	*		*		
Stop and jot	*	*	*		*		
Guided notes	*	*	*		*		*
Response cards/response slates	*	*	*		*		*
Hand signals	*	*	*		*		
Turn and talk	*			*	*	*	
Cued retell	*			*			*
Numbered heads together	*			*		*	*
Four corners	*			*		*	*
Snowball	*			*		*	*
Classroom mingle	*			*	*	*	*

SECTION 1

Verbal Engagement Strategies

Verbal engagement strategies all involve prompts that lead to students providing a verbal response to the teacher/class. These may be in the form of a single word, a concise description, or a longer discussion. There are four key ways in which verbal engagement strategies can be used.

1. Whip around
2. Quick poll
3. Choral responding
4. Individual questioning

Whip Around

Image source: unsplash.com/NeONBRAND

The whip around is a great way to involve all students quickly and is a great strategy for starting out a lesson by getting everyone's attention on the topic at hand. It can be used for activities such as priming background knowledge on a subject prior to a lesson or summarizing information learned at the end of a lesson, or as a brainstorming activity.

BIG IDEA

The teacher asks a question with many possible answers and then quickly prompts every student in the room to respond. For example, the teacher may ask students to name a U.S. state, then go up and down rows asking each student to either name a state that has not been named or pass. Similarly, the teacher can ask students to name their favorite book or to state one thing they learned from a previous lesson.

Step-by-Step Directions for Use

The whip around requires only an initial explanation so that students understand the routine. It is generally used in a planned manner but can also be unplanned.

1. Teach students the whip around routine.
   - Let them know that it is okay to say "pass" or to say, "Someone else took my answer."
   - Name the routine "whip around" or something similar so that they know when the activity is about to begin.
   - Make students aware that guessing—that is, making up an answer—is okay; this is not a test.
   - Practice with students a few times so that they understand the simple procedure.

2. Plan to use the whip around at the beginning of a lesson and for review.
   - Plan for responses that are very brief or even a single word.
   - Start at different points in the room—not always with the same student going first or last.
   - Remember that the purpose is to engage students and not to stump or shame them.

3. Provide reminders to students immediately before using the strategy: "We are getting ready to do a whip around."

4. After providing the prompt, quickly point to each student in succession, keeping the responses coming to quickly move through the entire classroom.
   - If a student does not respond, remind them that they can pass.
   - If a student does not respond with even a pass, move on quickly, and speak privately to the student afterward.

CONSIDERATIONS AND DIFFERENTIATION FOR FACE-TO-FACE ENVIRONMENTS

- Remember to keep the responses simple; long responses create a lengthy downtime for most students while awaiting their turn or the end.

- Teach students with cognitive challenges or content area deficits to listen to other students for clues before responding and that it is okay to say that someone else gave your answer (or to pass).

- Present from the front of the room so that all students can see when the teacher points to them to indicate their turn.

STEP INTO THE FACE-TO-FACE CLASSROOM

When planning an upcoming unit on the Civil War, Mr. Blake decided to use the whip around strategy to prime students' background knowledge on the subject. This would not only encourage all students to participate but also allow him to formatively assess what they knew about the subject. At the beginning of class, Mr. Blake displayed the question on the board: "What do you know about the Civil War?" He asked the students to jot down one thing they knew about the Civil War and be ready to give a response aloud. His only stipulation was that it needed to be short enough to fit on a bumper sticker. After giving the students adequate wait time, Mr. Blake explained,

> We are now going to go around the room, and when I point to you, you will give your bumper sticker answer. If you do not have an answer, don't worry. All you have to do is say "pass." Okay, we'll start from the back of the room and work across.

Mr. Blake was pleased to see that most of the students participated, with only a few who "passed" instead of giving an answer. He determined that he would use the strategy again at the end of the unit to summarize what they had learned.

CONSIDERATIONS AND DIFFERENTIATION FOR VIRTUAL ENVIRONMENTS

- Remember to keep the responses simple; long responses are especially difficult in terms of holding student attention when they are watching online.

- Teach students with cognitive challenges or content area deficits to listen to other students for clues before responding and that it is okay to say that someone else gave your answer (or to pass).

- Realize that each student may see the classroom arrangement differently on their own computer, so it may not be possible to have students respond by row or in natural order. The teacher should call out student names to prompt the next response and have it appear to be random.

- It is best if the teacher has the ability to control student microphones so that they can be on mute but unmuted as the student is called on. However, this is not always possible, and in such cases the teacher must provide reminders to students about unmuting and muting as they are called on.

STEP INTO THE VIRTUAL CLASSROOM

Ms. Slone sees her students in a grid formation that is unique to her computer. As the class meeting begins, she welcomes the students and briefly reminds them of the daily schedule and impending due dates. She then provides a very brief overview of what they have most recently covered in class, pivoting directly to the students and asking each to think of one fact learned about the U.S. Senate. She reminds all that she will call out names randomly and that everyone has the option of passing if they are unable to think of anything different from what has already been said. She prompts all the students about unmuting and then moves to the first student: "Remember to unmute when I call on you. Sam, you're up first; what have you got for us?" Sam is familiar with the routine and is able to quickly make a statement: "There are 100 senators." She thanks him for the response and works randomly, calling students from her class list, making a checkmark by each name as they respond. "Julie, what fact did you think of?" Julie hesitates and responds with a question: "Is the fact that the vice president breaks a tie something about the Senate?" "Yes, great," Ms. Bailey responds. Afterward, she noted that one student had passed and one had an answer that was slightly off base. She determined that she would follow up individually with these students later to see if additional help might be needed.

ADVANTAGES/DISADVANTAGES

One big advantage of the whip around strategy is that it engages all students individually in a very quick manner. It is especially good for getting students oriented to a lesson at the start of class or for providing an engaging review at the end of a lesson. One disadvantage is that it can be somewhat time-consuming and not something easy to use repeatedly. In addition, the whip around does not require students to think about the content as much as some other strategies. They often can get by with a simple "pass" statement or can easily recall something to say even if they did not understand it. For these reasons the whip around is generally more appropriate for social studies, humanities, and other content where open-ended questions make sense.

Quick Poll

Similar to the whip around strategy, the quick poll is a great way to actively engage all students individually in a quick and efficient manner. It can be used for activities such as priming background knowledge on a subject prior to a lesson or summarizing information learned at the end of a lesson, or as a brainstorming activity.

BIG IDEA

The teacher poses a question or prompt that has many possible answers and then "polls" the classroom by randomly calling on students, writing their answers on the board, and asking if others had the same answer. This process will continue until all student answers are given. Although not all students will verbally state an answer, they will need to be actively listening to the other students' responses. This strategy is useful across all grade levels and content areas.

Step-by-Step Directions for Use

Quick poll requires minimal teacher preparation. Although this strategy can be used in both a planned and an unplanned manner, preplanning the questions/prompts to be given to students is suggested. Questions/prompts can be delivered before, during, and after the lesson. Although no student materials are required, a writing instrument (e.g., pencil, pen, dry-erase marker) and writing surface (e.g., paper, response slate) may be used to write down responses.

1. Stop at a predetermined time in the lesson, and introduce the quick poll procedures.
   - Initially, explicitly teach and model the step-by-step process as well as expectations.
   - As students become familiar with the process, briefly review procedures and expectations.
2. Present students with a prompt/question.
3. After presenting the question/prompt, tell students how much time they will have to think of a response.
   - Although the length of wait time will depend on the question prompt given and the age of the student, three to four minutes is suggested.
   - Provide clear and consistent cues for how much time is available. This can include using a visual timer or verbally stating increments of time (e.g., "You have one more minute to finish your thought").
4. Monitor students as they write their responses, and provide assistance when needed.
5. Randomly call on three to four students, and write their answers on the board.
6. Read each answer, ask the students with the same answer to raise their hand, and record the number of students next to the answer.
7. Ask the students with responses that are not written on the board to raise their hand, and record these responses on the board.
8. Once all the responses are recorded, facilitate a whole-group discussion on the responses.
9. Provide specific feedback related to both the content of the responses and participation in the quick poll procedure.

CONSIDERATIONS AND DIFFERENTIATION FOR FACE-TO-FACE ENVIRONMENTS

- Remember to keep responses short and simple; longer responses will increase the downtime for most students while awaiting their turn or the end.

- Consider having students write their responses down or choose from a list of choices to increase the pace of the activity.

- Consider interspersing questions throughout to have students clarify their response, justify their thinking, or compare their response with those of others.

- Consider explicitly teaching students how to be effective listeners and speakers. This may include instruction on turn taking, speaking clearly, and appropriate feedback.

- Consider using visuals such as anchor charts to initially teach the strategy and later as a reminder for students.

- Provide assistance to students who have difficulties with processing information.

STEP INTO THE FACE-TO-FACE CLASSROOM

In an effort to immediately focus her students' attention on the mathematics lesson after small-group reading, Ms. Donita decided to use the quick poll strategy for students to identify quadrilaterals in the classroom. The first step in planning for the activity was to write down the prompt "Find a closed shape that has four straight sides" on chart paper, along with a few visual examples.

When the small-group reading time ended, Ms. Donita displayed the chart paper with the prompt and asked the students to look around the classroom as they transitioned back to their desks and find a closed shape that had four straight sides. She asked the students not to share what they found with the others. To provide additional support, she pointed to each example she had written on the chart paper and explicitly explained why it was an example.

(Continued)

(Continued)

To start the lesson, Ms. Donita asked for all students to give her a thumbs up if they had found a closed shape that had four sides. Once she saw that all students had their thumbs up, she then randomly selected one student to share their response. When the student replied, "My book," Ms. Donita replied, "Yes, a book has four straight sides. Good job!" and wrote the word book on a blank sheet of chart paper. She then prompted four more students to give their responses and wrote each of the responses on the chart paper. The chart paper included the following responses: book, paper, calendar, tile, and door. She then asked if any students had a similar response for each. For example, she said, "Raise your hand if you also had 'book' as your answer." Four students raised their hands, and Ms. Donita put a 5 next to the word book. She continued this process for the remaining four words. Finally, she asked the students to raise their hand if they had responses that were not written on the board. Four students raised their hand, and she added their responses to the chart paper.

To wrap up the activity, Ms. Donita briefly reviewed the properties of the shapes again and explained that these shapes are called quadrilaterals. Looking around at the students, she could see that all the students were engaged in the lesson.

Image source: https://unsplash.com/@kellysikkema

CONSIDERATIONS AND DIFFERENTIATION FOR VIRTUAL ENVIRONMENTS

- Remember to keep the responses short and simple. Shorter responses will increase the pacing, which is important in the virtual environment.

- Consider interspersing questions throughout to have students clarify their response, justify their thinking, or compare their response with those of others.

- Consider combining this strategy with the colored choice response card strategy (see Section 2), where students will show a specific color if they have the same answer as the one given (e.g., a green card), a different color if their answer has already been written down (e.g., blue), and another color if their answer has not yet been given (e.g., red).

- Consider using a classroom response system that will allow you to poll students, or create a word cloud.

STEP INTO THE VIRTUAL CLASSROOM

Ms. Allen decided to use the quick poll strategy to quickly and efficiently assess student comprehension of the video. In preparation for the lesson, she typed the following prompt on a word document: "In one to two words, name one way we use water."

During the lesson, Ms. Allen showed the three- to five-minute video to the students. After the video, she displayed the prompt on the computer screen and said,

> Now I am going to ask you to think of one way we can use water. Remember, your response should only be one to two words. When you have your answer, I want you to hold up your green response card.

When Ms. Allen noticed that all the students were displaying their green cards, she then randomly selected five students to share their response. She typed the following responses on the word document: to drink, to grow food, to cook, to clean, and to water grass. She then asked for any students having similar responses to raise their green response card. For example, she said, "Raise your green card if you also had 'to drink' as your answer." Ten students raised their green cards, and Ms. Donita typed a 10 next to "to drink." She continued this process for the remaining four words. Finally, she asked the students to raise their green card if they had responses that were not given. Two students raised their green cards, and she added their responses to the word document.

Ms. Allen wrapped up the activity by reviewing the ways in which people use water and transitioned into topics of water sustainability and the environmental issues introduced in the video. Overall, she was pleased to see how this activity helped students to be actively engaged while also allowing her to quickly assess student comprehension.

ADVANTAGES/DISADVANTAGES

One big advantage of the quick poll is that it engages all students individually in a very quick and efficient manner. Although not all students will verbally state an answer, they will need to be actively listening to the other students' responses. One disadvantage is that it can be somewhat time-consuming and not something you would implement on a consistent basis. In addition, students whose answers are already listed might become disengaged while other students are giving their responses.

Choral
Responding

STEP INTO THE
FACE-TO-FACE CLASSROOM

Ms. Naher is an upper-elementary resource teacher. In one of her co-taught classrooms, she works with a small group of students who are working to master basic math facts. While she knows that continued instruction on these facts is necessary, she is also under pressure to move through the standards-based content to fractions. She is looking to find a quick way to cover math facts while continuing to introduce new content on fractions.

STEP INTO THE
VIRTUAL CLASSROOM

Mr. Orr teaches a Drivers' Education class online to 14- and 15-year-old students who are preparing to apply for learners' permits. He enjoys the engaging conversations that he is able to generate with the students, but he is also aware that there are some very basic facts they will have to master if they are to pass their permit examinations. Mr. Orr wants to provide some repetitive practice for these facts but is afraid of losing student interest if the pace of the lesson is too slow.

Choral responding is simply verbal responses provided simultaneously as a group of students. While this strategy is often believed to be used only in very structured small-group direct-instruction lessons, the application is much broader.

Image source: unsplash.com/JeswinThomas

BIG IDEA

Choral responding involves a teacher query delivered to a group or full classroom, with the response by the group being in a simultaneous chorus, often signaled by a teacher prompt. For example, the teacher reminds the class that they need to check their answers in order to be finished with a mathematics problem, then asks, "So everyone, a mathematics problem is not done until you have what?" The teacher then points to the group, and they simultaneously respond, "Checked our answer." Similarly, the teacher can ask a small group of students, "What word do we use when we want to ask someone for something politely?" The students then respond in unison, "Please."

Step-by-Step Directions for Use

Choral responding requires an initial explanation and then frequent practice to keep the responses coming in unison. In addition, teacher prompts are likely necessary to facilitate tight choral responding.

1. Teach students the choral responding routine.
   - Specifically, teach both the signal and the desired response format.
   - Practice with students a few times so that they understand the simple procedure.

2. Plan to use choral responding to help students focus on important concepts that need to be fresh on their mind.
   - Use choral responding repetitively to help students commit concepts to memory.
   - Use choral responding in an unplanned manner to keep students focused on the lesson topic.

3. Provide reminders to students immediately preceding the use of this strategy: "We're getting ready to do a choral response."

4. After providing the question or request, demonstrate in some manner that you are about to provide a signal.
   - The signal can be verbal: "So it is called a what?"
   - The signal can be a hand gesture, a nod, or other physical prompt.

5. Observe the student responses, and make note of those who did not respond or responded incorrectly.

CONSIDERATIONS AND DIFFERENTIATION FOR FACE-TO-FACE ENVIRONMENTS

- Remember to keep the desired responses simple and succinct.

- Consider pairing students with cognitive deficits with a peer tutor who can help with appropriate responding in these instances.

- Present from the front of the room so that all students can see the teacher's prompt.

- When errors are heard, it may be appropriate to first repeat the correct answer aloud, explain why it is correct, and then immediately repeat the choral response activity.

STEP INTO THE FACE-TO-FACE CLASSROOM

Ms. Naher decides to incorporate choral response into her daily lessons. She explains to the students that she will pose a question and give them time to think. She tells them to wait for her signal "Everyone?" before responding in unison. Ms. Naher practices with the students by asking them questions like "What time does the bell ring to go home?" She praises them for waiting and responding in unison. She begins the lesson on fractions, embedding questions on math facts when appropriate. As she explains adding the numerators of the fractions, she provides her first choral response: "I need to add the numerators 4 and 6. What is 4 + 6? . . . Everyone?" The students respond "10" in unison. Ms. Naher quickly provides behavior-specific praise for waiting and feedback that their answer is correct. She then provides two more quick opportunities to respond. She is pleased that all of the students remain engaged and provide responses.

CONSIDERATIONS AND DIFFERENTIATION FOR VIRTUAL ENVIRONMENTS

- Remember to keep the desired responses simple and succinct.

- Consider providing fact sheets or other cues for students with cognitive deficits or other students who have difficulty with quick recall.

Image source: unsplash.com/AnnieSpratt

- Present from the front of the room so that all students can see the teacher's prompt.

- When errors are heard, it may be appropriate to first repeat the correct answer aloud, explain why it is correct, and then immediately repeat the choral response activity.

- It is best if the teacher has the ability to control student microphones so that they can be unmuted as a group prior to each choral response. However, this is not always possible, and in such cases the teacher must provide reminders to students about unmuting prior to each choral response.

STEP INTO THE VIRTUAL CLASSROOM

Mr. Orr decides to use choral responding with his online Drivers' Education class. As he continues leading students through the drivers' manual and covering new material, he finds multiple opportunities to remind them of key facts. For example, as the lesson content turns to adjustments for hazardous conditions, Mr. Orr uses a quick choral response regarding the position of hands on the steering wheel. "Let's do a quick choral response, unmute yourself; it is especially important to do this under hazardous conditions, but what position should your hands be on the wheel at all times?" Mr. Orr looks directly into his computer camera and points his finger as a signal, on which the entire class responds in unison, "2 and 10." Mr. Orr replies with a strong "Yes!" and continues into the lesson on hazardous road conditions. With each new content area, Mr. Orr finds it easy to sneak in opportunities for choral responding to key facts from previous chapters in the manual.

ADVANTAGES/DISADVANTAGES

One big advantage of choral responding is that it is very quick and easy to use in an unplanned manner. Oftentimes a teacher may realize that some particular fact or concept is difficult for students to remember. In these instances, providing multiple opportunities to chorally respond can help build the repetition necessary for maintaining this critical knowledge. The disadvantage is that the types of responses are limited to what can be provided verbally in a quick word or phrase. Choral responding is not appropriate for longer answers or deep open-ended questions. Some online classroom platforms may not allow more than one student at a time to respond. In these cases choral responding is not possible, and nonverbal responses may be an appropriate alternative for accessing quick group responses.

Individual Questioning Strategies For Student Response

Individual questioning techniques are perhaps the most common engagement strategy used by teachers. Questions are common because they are easy to use—on a whim we can just blurt them out as we go. While everyone is familiar with questioning, consideration of some basic principles can make this strategy as effective as it is easy to use.

Image source: unsplash.com/@nci

BIG IDEA

Individual students respond to teacher queries verbally by providing a factual response to a very specific question or stating an opinion to a more open-ended question. These questions can be simple or complex and can be focused on academics, behavior, or any topic of choice. For example, the teacher may ask a student to answer a simple question: "Sandy, what's the capital of Oregon?" Or the teacher may make this more complex by asking, "Sandy, how did Oregon decide where to put their capital?" Similarly, the teacher may ask a student to state an opinion simply by asking, "Stan, do you agree that level zero is the right voice level in the hall?" Or in a more complex manner the teacher may ask, "Stan, why do you think it's important for us to use a level-zero voice in the hall?" Note that in each case the question is directed to a specific student and not to the group at large.

Step-by-Step Directions for Use

While questioning can be used in a planned or unplanned manner, to be most effective, questioning requires more planning and forethought than one might think. Importantly, questioning by itself is not recommended as the sole manner of engaging students. First, it's hard to get high rates of responding across the classroom when queries are targeted only to individual students. Second, questioning can be slow while the teacher waits for an individual student to respond and then

(Continued)

(Continued)

potentially can take longer if the student's response requires correction. Unplanned individual questioning, on the other hand, can be implemented at any time just to keep the pace of instruction going. Regardless of the type of individual questioning strategy being used, it is important to remember that the purpose of this questioning is engagement more than evaluation. As such, the goal is to ask questions that can be correctly answered by students during 80% to 90% of trials.

1. Think ahead as to what questions will be most useful in driving instruction.
   - Create a mix of simple and complex questions.
   - Create a mix of closed- and open-ended questions.
   - Write down your questions so that you can refer to them at the right point during the lesson.

2. Start with questions for review.
   - Begin with questions delivered to the group, asking for volunteers and calling on someone who raises a hand.
   - Move toward questions that are directed at specific students.
   - Ask specific students to answer questions about what they already know.
   - As this strategy is used to kick off the lesson, keep the questions simple to keep it moving.
   - Find students who are sometimes reluctant to engage, and ask very basic questions that you believe can be answered correctly—this creates momentum.

3. As new content is introduced, use very simple and concrete individual questions to build momentum before moving to more complex questions.
   - Refer to lesson plans regarding when and what questions are appropriate during the lesson.
   - Ask no more than one individual question for every five OTRs provided to the group.
   - Avoid asking complex questions of students who you believe have anxiety with answering in front of the group.

4. Immediately correct the errors in responses.
   - As a rule of thumb, the teacher should be the one who delivers the corrections.
   - Avoid protracted correction of an individual student's errors in front of the class.
   - Deliver correction in a positive manner, prompting the student to get the correct answer.

CONSIDERATIONS AND DIFFERENTIATION FOR FACE-TO-FACE ENVIRONMENTS

- Use unplanned individual questions for the student who is engaged and attending but makes off-task comments.

  - Think of these students as being off task *within the lesson*, and take advantage of the fact that they are still attending.

  - Use off-task comments as an invitation to ask a relevant question—not as a punishment but one that can be easily answered to bring the student back to task.

- Questions to the group for volunteers and to specific individuals can be mixed, but questions to the group can be used to get an idea of what content might be more challenging (fewer hands raised).

- Teach students with cognitive challenges or content area deficits that it is okay to pass or to say, "I don't know."

  - Avoid singling out students with severe anxiety and those with more pronounced deficits, as questioning in this manner may be punitive.

- Move about the room while using individual questions so that interaction is more personal rather than always from the teacher at the front of the room.

STEP INTO THE FACE-TO-FACE CLASSROOM

Mr. Martinez explains to the students that he will read a small section of a story and then pause and ask some questions, so they should be ready. He has thought ahead of time about which students might be the best recipients for specific questions and which students might be best for answering the follow-up "Is that right?" questions. For example, he knows that Preston is a bright student but does not like to be put on the spot in front of

(Continued)

(Continued)

the class. While reading the first section of the story, a girl named Sarah is identified as the main character in the story, and the story is set in the mountains of Colorado. After reading the first section, Mr. Martinez calls on an individual student, Thomas, who is widely considered to be among the brightest in the room. "Thomas, when I snap my fingers, I want you to tell me the name of the main character in the story." After waiting a few seconds, he snaps his fingers while making eye contact with Thomas. Thomas replies verbally saying, "Sarah." He immediately turns to Preston and asks, "Thomas says 'Sarah'; Preston, do you agree?" Preston replies, "Yes." Mr. Martinez provides both students with verbal praise for the correct response. Mr. Martinez then follows up by asking another student about the setting of the story, following the same procedure. In this manner Mr. Martinez is able to get Preston to be individually engaged and receive public praise for his engagement.

CONSIDERATIONS AND DIFFERENTIATION FOR VIRTUAL ENVIRONMENTS

- Use unplanned individual questions for the student who does not appear to be attending to his or her computer.
  - Use off-task student comments as an invitation to ask a relevant question—not as a punishment but one that can be easily answered to bring the student back to task.
- Questions to the group for volunteers and to specific individuals can be mixed, but questions to the group can be used to get an idea of what content might be more challenging (fewer responses).
- Teach students with cognitive challenges or content area deficits that it is okay to pass or to say, "I don't know."
  - Avoid singling out students with severe anxiety and those with more pronounced deficits, as questioning in this manner may be punitive.
  - Remember that the purpose of individual questions is more about engagement than assessment—although there is always some degree of assessment possible.

- Be thoughtful in terms of who is asked to answer individually, and make it random so that it does not appear that you are calling on favorites or picking on anyone.

- Remember that students very likely will have their microphones muted and when called on will begin answering without sound. It's a good idea to always provide a visual or auditory prompt about unmuting when asking questions.

STEP INTO THE VIRTUAL CLASSROOM

Ms. Bailey continues to use choral responding and some cued retell with her students as she reviews content on the 12 keys of music. She begins asking for volunteers to answer more specific questions: "Who can tell me what the black keys on a piano play: Raise your hand if you remember. I see a few hands. How about Robert? Please unmute yourself, and tell us what your answer is." Robert responds, "The flat and sharp notes." Ms. Bailey quickly provides praise and then goes to a student, Angie, in whom she has less confidence. However, Ms. Bailey knows that Angie has already heard part of the answer, so there is a much better chance that she will be correct. "Angie, if it's true that the black keys play the flat and sharp notes, which notes are played by the white keys on a piano? Remember to unmute." Angie unmutes and responds, "The natural notes." This is correct, and Ms. Bailey provides Angie with praise: "Very good, Angie, you are correct, and you were right on top of the question." Ms. Bailey now has had an individual interaction with Angie, has engaged Angie, and has had an opportunity to provide her with praise.

Image source: https://unsplash.com/@thomascpark

ADVANTAGES/DISADVANTAGES

Of course, the big advantage of individual questioning is that the teacher can get a very strong engagement one-on-one with a student. There is also an opportunity for a personal interaction with the student, providing an opportunity for the teacher to initiate a positive relationship. While the purpose is engagement, there is also the possibility of getting an index of a student's knowledge or understanding of the lesson. Despite these advantages, the disadvantages related to individual questioning are perhaps greater than with any other engagement strategy. First, as has been noted, individual questioning is slow. In a class with larger numbers of students individual questioning as the sole strategy would likely mean that each student gets only one chance to respond during class. Thus, this strategy is best used sparingly and interspersed with other strategies allowing for higher rates of student response. Second, individual questioning puts students on the spot in front of their peers. While some students do not mind this, others may have extreme anxiety over such potential embarrassment. In such circumstances this strategy may actually cause students to be less engaged or even to defy the teacher's query out of fear. It is important to both use these individual questions in a measured manner and be thoughtful about how specific students may respond. Remember, the primary purpose of the individual question as an OTR is to engage students, not to evaluate them.

SECTION 2

Nonverbal Engagement Strategies

Nonverbal engagement strategies involve prompts that lead to students providing a response through the use of manipulatives, a written product, or an action. The nonverbal response may be as simple as a signaling gesture or a written response from single words to longer descriptions. There are four key ways in which nonverbal engagement strategies can be used:

1. Stop and jot

2. Guided notes

3. Response cards

4. Hand signals

Stop and Jot

Image source: unsplash.com/santivedri

Stop and jot, also known as the pause procedure or think and write, is a strategy that allows the teacher to break up lectures by having students respond in writing to teacher prompts. These prompts can include having students summarize content that was just presented, answer comprehension questions, apply information to a real-world context, or share their thoughts and opinions on a topic.

BIG IDEA

Students write a brief response to a teacher prompt. This brief pause in the lesson allows students to think about what they have learned while giving the teacher an opportunity to assess student understanding. Although this strategy can be useful across all grade levels and content areas, it is especially effective for higher grades, where the amount of teacher talk increases.

Step-by-Step Directions for Use

Stop and jot requires minimal teacher preparation. Although this strategy can be used in both a planned and an unplanned manner, preplanning the questions/prompts to be given to students is suggested. Questions/prompts can be delivered before, during, and after the lesson. Students will only need a writing instrument (e.g., pencil, pen, dry-erase marker) and a writing surface (e.g., paper, response slate, stop-and-jot graphic organizer).

1. Inform students at the beginning of the lesson that there will be times during the lesson when they will need to jot down responses to questions.

   - Model the strategy with students by answering a prompt/question using the writing procedure of your choice.

   - Explain to students that the answer does not need to be long (e.g., one to two sentences) and not to worry about spelling or grammar.

2. Stop at a predetermined time in the lesson, and present students with a prompt/question.

   - Questions at the beginning of the lesson could be used to activate prior knowledge or to assess prerequisite skills.

   - Questions/prompts during the lesson could be used to assess student understanding of the material and clarify misconceptions.

   - Questions/prompts after the lesson could be used to review critical aspects of the content learned, make connections to content previously learned, and provide relevance to the content learned.

3. After presenting a question/prompt, tell students how much time they will have to write responses.

   - Although the length of wait time will depend on the question prompt/given and the age of the student, three to four minutes is suggested.

   - Provide clear and consistent cues for how much time is available. This can include using a visual timer or verbally stating increments of time (e.g., "You have one more minute to finish your thought").

(Continued)

(Continued)

4. Monitor students as they write their responses, and provide assistance when needed.

5. Have students share their responses to the question/prompt by asking for volunteers, selecting specific students to model correct responses, or randomly selecting students.

6. Provide specific feedback related to both the content of their responses and participation in the stop-and-jot procedure.

CONSIDERATIONS AND DIFFERENTIATION FOR FACE-TO-FACE ENVIRONMENTS

- Consider providing fewer, simpler stop-and-jot opportunities for younger students that may include drawing pictures or symbols instead of writing.

- Consider having students write their responses on post-it notes and then place it on chart paper labeled "Parking Lot."

- Consider combining with the turn-and-talk strategy (see Section 3), where students will share their written responses with a partner before sharing with the class.

- Consider combining with the guided notes strategy (see next strategy), where students will fill in the blanks with key concepts, facts, or definitions.

- To save paper, consider having students jot their responses on response slates (see Section 3, pp. 68–71).

- Provide assistance to students who have difficulties with processing information. This could involve giving them sentence starters or providing them with questions/prompts in advance.

- Provide assistance to students who have difficulties with writing. This could include the use of voice-to-speech software or providing a scribe.

STEP INTO THE
FACE-TO-FACE CLASSROOM

Mr. Albini decided to use the stop-and-jot strategy to break up long readings during a book study on *Fahrenheit 451* by Ray Bradbury. For the first lesson Mr. Albini targeted the first seven pages of the book because it contains a lot of figurative language that may be difficult for his students to understand. He then created three short comprehension questions that the students could answer after every few pages.

During the reading Mr. Albini stopped after the second page and said,

> Now we are going to do a stop and jot. I am going to ask you a question, and I want you to jot down an answer. It does not have to be that long, only a sentence or two. And you don't need to worry about correct spelling or grammar. I just want you to get your thoughts down on paper. How does Montag describe the books on pages one and two, and what does this suggest? Take two to three minutes to jot down your response.

As the students were writing down their responses, Mr. Albini circulated the room to help those needing assistance. After three minutes, he randomly called on students to read their responses and asked follow-up questions to other students. He then continued the same process by reading a few pages, asking a question, having students stop and jot a response, and then calling on students to share what they had written. Although some students needed more prompting than others to write a response, he was encouraged that all students were actively participating in the lesson.

CONSIDERATIONS AND DIFFERENTIATION FOR VIRTUAL ENVIRONMENTS

- Consider interspersing brief, simpler stop-and-jot responses (i.e., 30 seconds) with longer stop-and-jot responses (three to four minutes).

- Consider using the strategy for both synchronous and asynchronous instruction.

- Provide assistance to students who have difficulties with processing information. This could involve giving them sentence starters.

- Provide accommodations to students who have difficulties with typing or processing information.

This could include modifying the activity so that students can record their responses orally (i.e., stop and say).

Image source: https://unsplash.com/@windows

ADVANTAGES/DISADVANTAGES

The greatest advantage of stop and jot is the opportunity to break up long lectures in order to decrease extended periods of teacher talk. Additionally, asking students to purposefully think about what they are learning promotes effective comprehension strategies as well as providing the teacher a method to formatively assess student learning throughout the lesson. All of this can be done with a minimal amount of planning, preparation, and resources. The one disadvantage of this strategy would be if the majority of your students require extended periods of time to process information or have difficulties with writing information in a timely manner. In these instances other strategies mentioned in this book may be more effective.

Guided Notes

STEP INTO THE
FACE-TO-FACE CLASSROOM

Ms. Casey is a second-grade teacher who is having difficulty keeping all students engaged with her lessons. With such a diverse group of students, she finds that her lessons are either too difficult for the lower-performing students or too easy for the higher-performing students. This has led to an increase in off-task behavior in both cases. She is looking for a strategy that would allow her to differentiate her instruction to engage more students.

STEP INTO THE
VIRTUAL CLASSROOM

Mr. Siva is teaching a high school biology class online. Part of his online instruction includes assigning readings from the textbook and then posting a video lecture that covers this content. However, he is growing concerned that the students are not getting the key information needed for the upcoming exam because they are not fully engaged in the videos by taking notes.

Image source: unsplash.com/dc

Guided notes are teacher-prepared handouts that have blank spaces for students to write in key facts or concepts. They provide students with a structured and purposeful way to attend to important concepts during instruction or independent reading assignments.

BIG IDEA

As a fact or concept is being introduced during instruction or an independent reading assignment, students fill in the missing information on the guided notes handout. This requires students to be actively engaged throughout the lesson while providing them an effective and efficient way to take notes on important information only. The completed notes can then be used as a study guide. Although this strategy can be useful across all grade levels and content areas, it is especially effective for higher grades, where the number of lectures and independent reading assignments increase.

Step-by-Step Directions for Use

There will be a moderate amount of teacher preparation for this strategy; therefore, we will discuss the preplanning process in the procedures below. Students will need the guided notes handout. The handout can be in either paper or digital format. Students will need a writing instrument (e.g., pencil, pen) if using the paper format and an electronic device (e.g., laptop) if using a digital format.

Preplanning

1. Review the upcoming lesson, and determine the most important information.
2. Using a word processor, create a document that contains the important information, and highlight keywords or phrases.
   - This can become your master document, which can be used as an answer key or to provide differentiation.
   - Format of guided notes can vary and include complete sentences, bulleted lists, and/or outlines.
3. Replace the highlighted keywords or phrases with underlined blanks.

Instruction

1. At the beginning of the lesson, distribute guided notes to students, and inform them that there will be times during the lesson when they will need to fill in one of the blanks.
2. Stop at predetermined times in the lesson, and prompt students to fill in their guided notes.
   - Initially, prompt students for every opportunity to fill in information.
   - As students become familiar with the process, gradually reduce the number of prompts they will receive.
3. Monitor students as they write their responses, and provide assistance when needed.
4. Have students share their responses with the class at the end of instruction to ensure completion and accuracy of the guided notes.
5. Provide specific feedback related to both the content of their responses and their participation in the guided notes process.

- When creating the guided notes, consider keeping the responses brief. Longer responses will increase the downtime for most students while waiting for others to complete.

- When creating the guided notes, make sure that response items are distributed throughout the lesson.

- Consider displaying guided notes on a screen or interactive whiteboard, and complete the guided notes along with the students.

- Consider differentiating the guided notes. Students who have difficulties with processing information or difficulties with handwriting may have notes that require limited writing, while others may have notes that require more writing.

STEP INTO THE FACE-TO-FACE CLASSROOM

Ms. Casey decided to incorporate guided notes into an upcoming lesson on punctuation. To prepare, she first created a lesson outline using digital presentation software that she would display on the classroom's interactive whiteboard. Next, she created a student handout template from the lesson outline. Finally, she created two separate guided notes handouts: one for students who struggle with writing and/or have difficulties processing information (see Figure 1 for guided notes example) and one for students who can write and/or process information fluently. Students who struggle would receive guided notes with relatively little writing and examples given, while other students would receive guided notes that would require more writing and would be asked to create their own examples.

At the beginning of the lesson, Ms. Casey handed out the differentiated guided notes and explained to students,

> I am handing out a page of notes that will help you with learning punctuation. You may notice that you have some blanks on your page. You are going to be filling in these blanks as we learn about periods, question marks, and exclamation marks. You don't have to worry about when to fill in the blanks. I will tell you as we get to it.

Ms. Casey continued her lesson on punctuation and stopped at pre-determined times so that the students could complete parts of their guided notes. For additional support she had the outline displayed on the board so that students could copy the information if needed. She was pleased to see that more students were engaged in the lesson and there were fewer occasions when she needed to redirect students for being off task. Additionally, she had the students put the guided notes in their folder so that they could use them as a reference in future practice activities and homework.

FIGURE 1 ● Guided notes example

GUIDED NOTES: Punctuation

PERIOD

    A.   _____: used to mark the end of a statement.

        a. *Example:* Tom was playing basketball.
        b. *Example:* Jill sits in the chair_

    A. Abbreviations

        a. Mister: _____
        b. Doctor: _____
        c. Street: _____
        d. Road: _____
        e. Avenue: _____
        f. Feet: _____

QUESTION MARK

    A. _____: used to mark the end of a question.

        a. *Example:* Where is the dog?
        b. *Example:* Who is that man_

EXCLAMATION MARK

    A. _____: used to mark the end of a strong feeling.

        a. *Example:* I had the best time!
        b. *Example:* That was a great shot_

CONSIDERATIONS AND DIFFERENTIATION FOR VIRTUAL ENVIRONMENTS

- When creating the guided notes, consider keeping the responses brief. Longer responses may lead to students missing key information because they are writing.

- Consider the format you will allow your students to use: handwritten or digital.
  - If asking students to hand write the notes, consider how they will be able to obtain the document.

    Image source: https://unsplash.com/ @surface
  - If asking students to type notes on a word processor, consider possible formatting issues that may occur.
- If teaching synchronously, consider displaying guided notes on your computer screen, and complete the guided notes along with the students.

STEP INTO THE VIRTUAL CLASSROOM

Mr. Siva thought that creating guided notes for his video lectures might help his students remember the key information needed for the exam. When planning for an upcoming video lecture on analyzing ecosystems, Mr. Siva thought of the key elements that he wanted his students to know from the lesson: abiotic and biotic components, producers, consumers, and decomposers. Next, he created guided notes that students could download and complete using their computer. Because the guided notes were to be completed digitally, he decided to put them in a table format so that students could easily type in information.

Mr. Siva then created his presentation using digital presentation software. This allowed him to incorporate presentation slides that would prompt students to fill in their guided notes. For example, one slide was titled "Guided Notes: What Is an Abiotic Component? What Are Some Examples of Abiotic Components?" Bullet points on the slide included information that students would need to add to the table.

- An abiotic factor is a nonliving part of an ecosystem that shapes its environment.
- Examples include the following:
  - Wind, sunlight, soil, water, atmosphere, and temperature

When recording the video, Mr. Siva told the students that they would need to complete the guided notes using the information on the slides and then submit the completed notes as an assignment.

After recording the video, Mr. Siva was confident that the students would be more engaged with the video. Not only would the guided notes require them to be actively engaged while watching the video, but also they would have a resource to use when studying for the exam.

ADVANTAGES/DISADVANTAGES

The greatest advantage of guided notes is that it promotes active engagement while providing an effective and efficient way to take notes on important information. Additionally, it is very easy to differentiate, so all students can be successful. Although this strategy is effective, it does require a moderate amount of time to create the guided notes handout. Furthermore, it may be difficult to implement if the majority of your students require extended periods of time to process information or have severe difficulties with writing information in a timely manner.

Response Cards

Response cards are simply small cards held by students that allow them to respond in a number of ways. There are several ways to use response cards to engage students during instruction.

- Colored choice
- Multiple choice
- True/false
- Response slates and whiteboards

RESPONSE CARDS: COLORED CHOICE

STEP INTO THE FACE-TO-FACE CLASSROOM

A ninth-grade social studies teacher, Mr. Buck, was preparing for a unit on basic economics. When he had previously taught this unit, he had noticed that students struggled with the vocabulary associated with economics, which greatly affected their understanding. He knew that he would need to preteach these vocabulary terms; therefore, his first lesson would be defining economic terms such as *scarcity*, *production*, *market*, and *cost*.

There are several ways to use response cards to engage students during instruction. Perhaps the simplest of these is the colored choice cards, which involves students having two or more colored cards representing various choices. The cards can be used to quickly survey student opinions or can be more closely tied to content questions.

BIG IDEA

Students respond to teacher queries by raising a colored card to indicate a choice or preference. For example, the teacher may ask students to raise their red cards if they wish to take a break now or a blue card if they wish to take a break in 10 minutes. Similarly, the teacher can ask students about the answer to a question with multiple choices by having each choice associated with a particular color of card.

Step-by-Step Directions for Use

The colored choice cards require very little setup and can be used in both a planned and an unplanned manner.

1. Deliver cards to students, and teach them how they are to be used.

    • Show students how to hold a choice card up to be seen.

    • Tell students that the color associated with choices will be designated for each opportunity, so they need to listen.

(Continued)

(Continued)

- Make students aware that guessing is okay—this is not a test.
- Practice with students a few times so that they understand the simple procedure.

2. Plan to use the cards at specific points during instruction.

- Determine what the choices will be.
- Make sure that the possible choices do not outnumber the available card colors.
- Use the cards to break up longer periods of teacher talk and surrounding new or complex content.
- Remember that the purpose is to engage students and not to stump them.

3. Provide reminders to students about colored choice cards immediately preceding their use: "We're getting ready to do a colored card choice, so have your cards ready."

4. After presenting a choice, wait for all the students to respond before moving on.

- If a student does not respond, provide one reminder/prompt.
- If a student does not respond after a prompt, continue with those who have responded, and speak privately to the student afterward.

5. Use students' attention as an opportunity to provide specific feedback related to both the content of their responses and their participation in the choice card process.

CONSIDERATIONS AND DIFFERENTIATION FOR FACE-TO-FACE ENVIRONMENTS

- Consider asking students to discuss choices with a partner or in groups before responding.
- Teach students with cognitive challenges or content area deficits to look to other students for clues before responding (this prevents fear of failure while still promoting engagement).
- Present choice opportunities while walking around the room rather than always from the front—gain proximity to students who are most likely to struggle with attention to such tasks.
- Consider ways to use this strategy in an unplanned and impromptu manner to get students' attention when not directly involved in content (indicate preference, understanding, etc.).

STEP INTO THE
FACE-TO-FACE CLASSROOM

To preteach the economic vocabulary, Mr. Buck decided to give the students statements related to the definitions and have them use colored choice cards to decide whether a statement is an example of the definition or a nonexample of the definition.

The first step in planning was to look at the definitions of each term and identify their critical attributes to make them more student friendly. For example, the student-friendly definition of scarcity is a situation where something is not easy to find or get. Mr. Buck went through the rest of the terms (i.e., goods, market, cost) and determined each term's critical attributes to create student-friendly definitions and then created examples and nonexamples for each. Finally, he purchased colored sticky notes: one yellow pad and one green pad.

To begin the lesson, Mr. Buck introduced the student-friendly definitions that he had displayed on a digital presentation slide. He then began to give each student a green and a yellow sticky note and explained,

> To help us better understand these terms, I am going to give you a statement and ask you if it is an example of this term or a nonexample of this term. If it is an example, you will hold up your yellow sticky note; if a nonexample, hold up your green sticky note. Because I want to give you a little time to think, don't raise your sticky note until I tell you.

Mr. Buck started with the term *scarcity*. He stated to the class,

> Okay, we know that scarcity is a situation where something is not easy to find or get. Now let us look at this statement. Each year a limited amount of the flu vaccine is available to the population, meaning that there is not enough for each individual to be vaccinated. Is this an example or a nonexample of scarcity? Think about it.

After five seconds, he prompted the students to raise their sticky notes. He then replied,

> Those that have their yellow sticky notes up are correct. This is an example of scarcity because there was not a sufficient amount of the resource to go around. Now, let us try another. I planted peppers in my garden, and I now have more than I can possibly eat. Think about it.

After five seconds, he prompted the students to raise their sticky notes. He then chose a student who had the correct answer and

(Continued)

(Continued)

asked, "Peter, why do you think this is a nonexample? Yes, you are correct. This is a nonexample of scarcity because there was more than a sufficient amount of the resource to go around." Mr. Buck continued this process for the terms *goods*, *market*, and *cost*.

Mr. Buck then checked the students' understanding of the terms by actively involving them in generating their own examples and nonexamples for each term. He did this by, first, having them work in pairs to generate multiple examples and nonexamples of the terms. Then, they introduced these examples and nonexamples to the class and had their classmates use their green and yellow sticky notes to determine whether it was an example or a nonexample of the term. By the end of the lesson, Mr. Buck was confident that the students had an initial understanding of the terms for the unit. Because this activity was so easy and efficient to implement, he decided to use it throughout the unit to serve as a brief review of the terms.

CONSIDERATIONS AND DIFFERENTIATION FOR VIRTUAL ENVIRONMENTS

- Consider using colored choice cards only in a synchronous environment to assess student learning in a quick, efficient manner. This strategy is not compatible with asynchronous learning.

- Because students will need to have the cards outside of the classroom, consider creating a set of laminated cards on a ring that can be delivered to the students' homes.

  - If this is not possible, teach students to make their own response cards and to keep them ready for use during each lesson.

  - To make sure that all students have cards for the lesson, ask students to have them with them for every lesson, or inform them that they will be needed in advance (e.g., included as materials needed for the weekly agenda).

- For younger students and/or virtual platforms without the hand-raising feature, consider having students use the cards when wanting to participate (e.g., display green if you have something to share).

- Consider using response cards to help with procedural routines such as raising a hand.

- Consider providing fact sheets or other cues for students with cognitive deficits or other students who have difficulty with quick recall.

STEP INTO THE
VIRTUAL CLASSROOM

Mr. Bachmann decided to use colored choice cards, with a green card representing a subject and the red card representing a verb. To prepare for the lesson, Mr. Bachmann selected words that represented the definitions the class had learned for both subject and verb, and wrote them on index cards. He also added in the weekly agenda that the students were to have their colored response cards he had previously given them on the day of the lesson.

To begin the lesson, Mr. Bachmann reviewed with the class the definitions they had previously learned for *subject* and *verb*. He pointed to the definitions typed on the computer screen and said,

> Today we are going to continue learning about subjects and verbs. We have learned that a subject is a person, place, thing, quality, or idea. On the other hand, a verb is a doing word that describes a body action or a mind action.

Mr. Bachmann prompted the students to get out their colored choice cards and said,

> To help us practice, I am going to give you a word that is either a subject or a verb. When I snap my fingers, I want you to show me the green side of the card if you think it is a subject and the red side of the card if you think it is a verb. Ready? The first word is *book*. Think about it.

Mr. Bachmann waited approximately five seconds and snapped his fingers to prompt the students to raise their cards. He quickly noticed that all the students were showing him their green cards. "Yes, it is a thing, which makes it a subject. Good job! Now put your cards down on your desk. The next word is *jump*. Remember, don't raise your card until I snap." After five seconds, he snapped his fingers and noticed that all the students raised their red cards. "Yes, it is a body action, which makes it a verb. Great job!"

As the activity continued and the words became more challenging for the students, Mr. Bachmann modified his routine. For example,

(Continued)

(Continued)

when he noticed that not all students had the correct answer for the word wish, he asked a student showing a red card why he thought it was a verb. When the student responded that it shows action, Mr. Bachmann replied,

> Yes, it is a doing word. Doing words are either a body action or a mind action. In this case it is a mind action. If you are unsure, ask yourself if you can do the word. If so, it is a verb. For example, can I wish? Yes! Then, it is a verb. On the other hand, can I happiness? No! Then, it is a subject.

Mr. Bachmann continued the same process of giving the students a word, allowing think time, prompting their response, and then asking an individual student to justify their thinking.

Overall, Mr. Bachmann was pleased with the colored choice card activity. He was able to increase student engagement while also assessing student understanding on subject and verb. Based on the success of this lesson, he reused the green/red cards when asking students true/false or yes/no questions.

ADVANTAGES/DISADVANTAGES

Of course, the big advantage of the colored choice response cards is that they are simple to use in both a planned and an unplanned manner. Students can keep the cards with them at all times, allowing the teacher to call for a response at any time it may be necessary to refocus the group. They are also easy to assess as the teacher needs only to glance for colors rather than read letters, numbers, or other more specific responses. The only disadvantage is that the choices are limited by the number of colored cards each student has available. Because having more than four different colors gets to be more challenging for the teacher, colored choice cards are probably best used for more binary choices (yes/no, choice 1/choice 2). Additionally, it may be challenging to make sure that all students have their cards in the virtual environment.

RESPONSE CARDS: MULTIPLE CHOICE

STEP INTO THE
FACE-TO-FACE CLASSROOM

Ms. Newton teaches an elementary classroom in a very rural setting. Her class is currently working on a science unit covering the solar system. The unit requires students to remember key facts and understand complex and abstract concepts. Ms. Newton is worried that her students do not have complete understanding of these facts and concepts. She feels that they need more repetition of the content. But the students have become restless, and she has begun to find it difficult to engage them throughout the lesson. She thinks that any form of repetition may be too boring and increase student off-task behavior.

STEP INTO THE
VIRTUAL CLASSROOM

Mr. Hand is teaching a world geography class online to a virtual classroom of high school students. He would really like to have his students answer chorally, but because of the online platform his district uses, he cannot hear all of the students at one time. He feels that he needs to have some way of keeping the students engaged while also assessing the degree to which the class as a whole is understanding the content he is teaching. He has thought about asking more questions of individual students, but he has found that it is too easy for students to simply answer with an "I don't know." This response tends to halt the lesson and provides no real information as he believes students answer in this manner simply to avoid being engaged.

 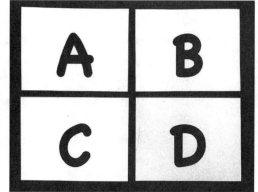

Students can be provided with multiple cards, each with a different choice for answering. These can be A, B, C, D; 1, 2, 3, 4; or even red, yellow, green, and blue. The idea is that when the teacher provides a prompt to respond, that prompt would ask students to decide among a range of possible responses and to hold up the card that represents their choice of the correct response.

BIG IDEA

Students respond to teacher queries by raising one of a number of cards that indicate different choices. For example, the teacher may point to a state on the map and ask students to respond with their multiple-choice cards whether the state's name is A = Arizona, B = Alaska, C = Alabama, or D = Arkansas. Each student then selects the card representing his or her choice and raises it for the teacher to view.

Step-by-Step Directions for Use

The colored choice cards require very little setup and can be used in both a planned and an unplanned manner.

1. Deliver cards to students, and teach them how they are to be used.
   - Show students how to hold a multiple-choice card up to be seen.
   - Tell students that the letter, number, or color associated with the choices will be designated for each opportunity, so they need to listen.
   - Make students aware that guessing is okay—this is not a test.
   - Practice with students a few times so that they understand the simple procedure.
2. Plan to use the cards at specific points during instruction.
   - Determine what the choices will be.
   - Make sure that the possible choices have one clear correct answer. Remember, this is for engagement and not to be used as a challenge.
   - Use this strategy to break up longer periods of teacher talk and surrounding new or complex content.
   - Remember that the purpose is to engage students and not to stump them.

3. Provide reminders to students about multiple-choice cards immediately preceding their use: "We are getting ready to do a multiple-choice card activity, so have your cards ready."

4. After presenting the choices, wait for all students to respond before moving on.

   - If a student does not respond, provide one reminder/prompt.

   - If a student does not respond after a prompt, continue with those who have responded, and speak privately to the student afterward.

5. Use students' attention to the card activity as an opportunity to provide specific feedback related to both the content of their responses and their participation in the choice card process.

CONSIDERATIONS AND DIFFERENTIATION FOR FACE-TO-FACE ENVIRONMENTS

- Consider asking students to discuss choices with a partner or in groups before responding.

- Teach students a strategy for having a process of elimination to select the most likely answer.

- Teach students with cognitive challenges or content area deficits to look to other students for clues before responding (this prevents fear of failure while still promoting engagement).

  - For younger students or those with language challenges consider using colors, animals, or other choices rather than letters or numbers.

- Present choice opportunities while walking around the room rather than always from the front—gain proximity to students who are most likely to struggle with attention to such tasks.

- Consider ways to use the strategy in an unplanned and impromptu manner to get students' attention when not directly involved in the content (indicate preference, understanding, etc.).

STEP INTO THE
FACE-TO-FACE CLASSROOM

Ms. Newton completes an explanation of how the planets' distance from the sun affects both their orbit time and their temperature. While the lesson was not particularly difficult and the students had opportunities to engage as a group, Ms. Newton decides to provide some opportunities to build in some repetition of the new content to be sure that the students are fluent with the information. All students have a set of small laminated response cards on their desk, each containing cards labeled A, B, C, and D. The routine for using the cards is familiar to the students as it was taught at the start of the year and used often. Ms. Newton provides a direction to the class: "Let us do some multiple-choice response cards to get us thinking more about what we have just learned. Have your cards ready, and I will give you the options." During planning, Ms. Newton had written out five different questions covering the new content, each with four multiple-choice answer options. She prompted the students to be ready: "Okay, here is the first question; show me that you have your response cards in your hand." She then projected the first question on the screen and read it aloud: "Which planet is closest to the sun? Is it A. Mercury, B. Venus, C. Earth, or D. Mars?" She continued with reminders to facilitate student responding: "Think about what we talked about today, and hold up the card that you think is the best answer." Once all the students had a card held up, she provided feedback;

> Wow, I see a lot of A. Mercury, and that is the right answer. Remember, we talked about how it was very hot because it was so close to the sun? Some people may have said Mars because it is called the Red Planet, but it is actually the farthest away of those four choices.

She then moved on to the next question using the same routine. In the end, Ms. Newton reviewed the content and gave the students directions for doing some group work building models of the solar system.

CONSIDERATIONS AND DIFFERENTIATION FOR VIRTUAL ENVIRONMENTS

- Consider using multiple-choice cards only in a synchronous environment, to assess student learning in a quick, efficient manner. This strategy is not compatible with asynchronous learning.

- Because students will need to have the cards outside of the classroom, consider creating a set of laminated cards on a ring that can be delivered to the students' homes (see page 50).

- ○ If this is not possible, teach students to make their own response cards and keep them ready for use during each lesson.

- ○ To make sure that all students have cards for the lesson, ask students to have them with them for every lesson, or inform them that they will be needed in advance (e.g., included as materials needed for the weekly agenda).

- Consider providing fact sheets or other cues for students with cognitive deficits or students who have difficulty with quick recall.

- Teach students a strategy for having a process of elimination to select the most likely answer.

- Consider ways to use the strategy in an unplanned and impromptu manner to get students' attention when not directly involved in the content (indicate preference, understanding, etc.).

STEP INTO THE VIRTUAL CLASSROOM

Mr. Hand provided a brief overview of some new content he had just presented on the world rivers. He then reminded the students that rivers were a major part of what would be studied during the current unit and asked whether there were any questions. He looked at his computer screen for a virtual hand raise but saw none. "Okay, looks like you all are feeling comfortable with this new information on world rivers, so let's do a little practice." Because using multiple-choice cards was a new routine for the classroom, he introduced it to the students and asked them to create their own cards.

I asked you all to have a piece of paper and fold it to create four squares. Now I want you to write the letter "A" in the first square—big enough to fill the square. Now do a B, C, and D in the other three squares—and remember to make them big enough to fill the square.

After giving a minute for the students to finish this process, he showed them how to hold the paper in different ways to show a single

(Continued)

(Continued)

letter. "Now, I have some questions about rivers that I am going to put up, and you can use your letter card to show me what you think are the correct answers." Mr. Hand then shared his screen to show the first question and read it aloud:

> We know the Amazon is the longest river in the world at more than 4,200 miles. What is the second longest? Is it A. the Mississippi, B. the Yangtze in China, C. the Nile in Egypt, or D. none of these? Hold up your card to indicate your answer—remember to hold it up so your camera can see it.

Once all the students had raised their cards, he provided feedback: "I see lots of different answers, but most of you are holding up a C—the Nile River—and that is correct." He then went on to provide further information while he had student attention on the topic, delivered in the form of a rhetorical question: "Are there any American rivers in the top 10? No, the Missouri River is the longest one in America, but it is not even in the top 10 for the world." Mr. Hand then shared the next question on his screen and repeated the procedure.

ADVANTAGES/DISADVANTAGES

As with other response cards, one big advantage of multiple choice response cards is that they are simple to use in both a planned and an unplanned manner. Students can keep the cards at their desks at all times, allowing the teacher to call for a response at any time it may be necessary to refocus the group. They are also easy to assess as the teacher needs only to glance for colors rather than read letters, numbers, or other, more specific responses. The slight disadvantage is that providing multiple choices and linking them to corresponding cards is more difficult to do in an impromptu manner. While it is not impossible to come up with a multiple-choice question off the cuff, the multiple-choice response cards are probably going to be more useful when preplanned.

RESPONSE CARDS: TRUE/FALSE

STEP INTO THE FACE-TO-FACE CLASSROOM

Mr. Cross is teaching psychology during the first period each day to a classroom of high school juniors and seniors. The students come into the classroom and get settled quickly, but their attention tends to fade if not continually engaged. Mr. Cross knows that the students tend to behave better when they are highly engaged in discussions, but he also needs to keep student attention to provide new content and to review important facts. He is concerned that if he uses too much class time with discussion, he will lose precious instructional time and will not able to cover all the material to the depth needed for students to pass the final exam.

STEP INTO THE VIRTUAL CLASSROOM

Ms. Sandwich has been teaching an online health class to a group of third-grade students. She finds that children of this age have a difficult time staying engaged with the lesson content, possibly because they are used to watching cartoons or playing video games when looking at a computer screen. She says it is hard to compete with that level of excitement and engagement while teaching health, and she is looking for a way to provide very quick and mostly unplanned opportunities for students to respond within the curriculum throughout the lesson.

The true/false option for response cards may seem like an option that could be used with either the colored choice or the multiple-choice cards, and in many respects, it is. But having specifically dedicated true and false cards does present some advantages over these other options because of how quickly they can be used without explanation or setup.

BIG IDEA

Students respond to teacher queries by raising a card to indicate either true or false (T or F). For example, the teacher may ask students to use their true/false cards to indicate whether they think a problem was done correctly, whether they agree with an answer, or even whether they agree with a statement made by the teacher. Because the true and false cards are self-explanatory, the teacher does not need to take the time to explain which card represents agreement and which represents disagreement.

Step-by-Step Directions for Use

The true or false cards require very little setup and can be used in both a planned and an unplanned manner.

1. Deliver cards to students, and teach them how they are to be used.
   - Show students how to hold a choice card up to be seen.
   - Call this "true or false" or some other name so that when this phrase is mentioned all the students know immediately what's coming next.
   - Briefly explain that the true card means that you agree and the false card means that you do not agree.
   - Make students aware that guessing is okay—this is not a test.
   - Practice with students a few times so that they understand the simple procedure.

2. Plan to use the cards at specific points during instruction.
   - Determine what the questions will be.
   - Make sure that the possible choices are clear and that there is a clear correct answer.
   - Use the strategy to break up longer periods of teacher talk and surrounding new or complex content.
   - Remember that the purpose is to engage students and not to stump them.

3. Provide reminders to students about the true and false cards immediately preceding their use: "Here comes a true or false question, so have your cards ready."

4. After presenting a true/false question, wait for all the students to respond before moving on.
   - If a student does not respond, provide one reminder/prompt.
   - If a student does not respond after a prompt, continue with those who have responded, and speak privately to the student afterward.

5. Use students' attention to the card activity as an opportunity to provide specific feedback related to both the content of their responses and their participation in the choice card process.

CONSIDERATIONS AND DIFFERENTIATION FOR FACE-TO-FACE ENVIRONMENTS

- With more challenging questions, consider asking students to discuss choices with a partner or in groups before responding.

- Teach students with cognitive challenges or content area deficits to look to other students for clues before responding (this prevents fear of failure while still promoting engagement).

- Present true/false response opportunities while walking around the room rather than always from the front—gain proximity to students who are most likely to struggle with attention to such tasks.

STEP INTO THE FACE-TO-FACE CLASSROOM

Mr. Cross has provided all the students in his classroom with a set of small laminated response cards attached by a ring. The cards include a single card with a "T" on one side and an "F" on the other. He has made it clear to all that the T and F card was to be used to indicate true or false and that students need to be ready as he may spring such a question on them at any time and require that they respond by holding up the correct side of their card. He goes through the process once as practice: "So if I suddenly yelled out 'true or false,' you would need to grab your card—and I might say, 'Freud was the father of psychoanalysis—true or false'." He then pulled out his own card and held up the T side, explaining, "You would all need to get to your cards fast and hold up your answer. I held up the T because this is a true statement." He then provided a real practice opportunity, yelling out "True or False" and waiting for student eyes, then making the statement "Carl Jung was a behaviorist" and immediately providing the reminder: "Hold up your card to indicate whether you think this is true or false. I'm seeing lots of F cards, and that's because this is false—we all know Jung was a disciple of Freud at one point." Now that the students had this routine down, Mr. Cross used it on a regular but random basis to keep the students engaged with the content. He also found over time that this routine was useful in getting a quick read on whether the students were understanding the concepts being discussed.

- Consider using the true or false strategy only in a synchronous environment, to assess student learning in a quick, efficient manner. This strategy is not compatible with asynchronous learning.

- Because students will need to have the cards outside of the classroom, consider creating a set of laminated cards on a ring that can be delivered to the students' homes.

  ○ If this is not possible, teach students to make their own response cards and to keep them ready for use during each lesson.

  ○ To make sure that all students have cards for the lesson, ask students to have them with them for every lesson, or inform them that they will be needed in advance (e.g., included as materials needed in the weekly agenda).

- Consider providing fact sheets or other cues for students with cognitive deficits or students who have difficulty with quick recall.

  ○ For younger students or those with language challenges, consider using colors, animals, or other choices rather than the letters "T" and "F."

- Present true or false response opportunities throughout the lesson rather than only at the end of a section.

STEP INTO THE VIRTUAL CLASSROOM

Because she could not immediately provide laminated cards to all her online students, Ms. Sandwich had all students create their own true or false cards as part of an activity. She led them through the simple process of using a piece of paper and had them write "Yes" on one side and "No" on the other because she liked asking, "Is this true?" rather than "True or false?" She then presented it to the students as a game. "I am going to say something that may be true or not true. When I ask, 'Is this true?' I want you to raise your card." As she described the rules,

Ms. Sandwich held up her own card. "Your job is to decide if what I said is true and answer by holding up your 'Yes' or your 'No' card." She provided an initial example:

> Maybe I would say to everyone, "Is this true?" and then say, "Germs are really big, and we can see them." If you heard that, you would think, no way, germs are small, so that is not true, and you would hold up your "No" card.

At this point she asked all the students to hold up their card so that she could make sure that all had one. Then, she provided a practice opportunity. "Hey, is this true? It is important to wash your hands before you touch food. Hold up the card you think is right." Once the routine was comfortable for the students, Ms. Sandwich used it frequently and randomly to keep student attention. She liked to mix this strategy with other similar response card strategies as a method of keeping students engaged with the health content.

ADVANTAGES/DISADVANTAGES

The one big advantage of the true or false cards in comparison with the other response cards is the simplicity of the choices and the fact that it can be applied with little or no explanation. Students can keep the cards at their desks at all times, allowing the teacher to call for a response at any time. In fact, the true or false cards is one of the quickest and simplest ways of getting all students to think and then respond physically. As with the other response cards, this method is also easy to assess as the teacher needs only to glance at the card responses. The only disadvantage is that the choices are limited to binary true or false questions. Over the course of a lesson, teachers will want to use a range of engagement strategies providing more rigorous content.

RESPONSE CARDS: RESPONSE SLATES AND WHITEBOARDS

STEP INTO THE
FACE-TO-FACE CLASSROOM

Ms. Chu is a co-teacher in a high school algebra class. She wants to keep her students engaged during class and monitor their progress before homework is assigned. While she prefers asking individual questions of students, she has found that this strategy alone is too slow to allow her to engage every student during class and still cover all the necessary material. She wants to find a strategy that would allow her to engage more students while still being able to see their work on specific problems.

STEP INTO THE
VIRTUAL CLASSROOM

Mr. Steele teaches language arts online to elementary students and is concerned that his students are disengaged during instruction. He typically works from a shared screen and diagrams sentences while describing how and why he diagrams. He realizes that diagramming sentences is not exciting for elementary students, but it is part of the required curriculum. Mr. Steele is looking for a way to have more interaction with the students in a manner that still allows him to get some form of information on how individual students perform

While response slates and whiteboards are not technically response cards, they do involve the same set of principles, in that students are required to consider a response and hold it up. We refer to this as a written response despite the fact that an action may be required because the student's answer to the question is written. In addition, it is also easy to create these by simply laminating a paper card so that it can be used with a dry-erase pen. The difference, of course, is that slates require the student to produce rather than select an answer. Cards and slates can be small enough to fit in the palm of a hand, tablet sized, or even in the shape of a small paddle with a small handle.

BIG IDEA

Students respond to teacher queries by writing on dry-erase cards, chalkboards, or erasable slates. Students can respond by drawing or writing, depending on the teacher's query. For example, the teacher may ask students to draw a pentagon on their slate and raise it up over their head. Similarly, the teacher can ask students to write a word that means the same as "flat" or to indicate which U.S. state has the most coastline.

Step-by-Step Directions for Use

Response slates and whiteboards require slightly more setup than other response card options, but they can still be used in both a planned and an unplanned manner.

1. Deliver erasable cards or slates to students, and teach them how they are to be used.

   - Show students how to hold the card or slate up to be seen.
   - Demonstrate that the card or slate is erasable and that they will be both writing and erasing them each time they are used.
   - Model appropriate use by allowing students to provide the query to which the teacher responds.
     - Model both drawn and written responses.
   - Make students aware that guessing is okay—this is not a test.
   - Practice with students a few times so that they understand the procedure.

(Continued)

(Continued)

2. Plan to use the cards or slates at specific points during instruction.
   - Determine what the directions will be.
   - Make sure that the possible choices can be easily drawn or written in no more than a few words.
   - Remember that the purpose is to engage students and not to stump them.

3. Provide reminders to students about response slates or whiteboards immediately preceding their use: "We're getting ready to use our whiteboards, so have them ready."

4. After presenting a query or direction, wait for all the students to respond before moving on.
   - If a student does not respond, provide one reminder/prompt.
   - If a student does not respond after a prompt, continue with those who have responded, and speak privately to the student afterward.

5. Use students' attention as an opportunity to provide specific feedback related to both the content of their responses and participation within the process.

CONSIDERATIONS AND DIFFERENTIATION FOR FACE-TO-FACE ENVIRONMENTS

- Consider using response slates or whiteboards early in the lesson to get students thinking and then later in the lesson to facilitate higher-order thinking.

- Consider asking students to discuss choices with a partner or in groups and respond jointly.

- Consider using response slates or whiteboards to initiate practice, so that students get opportunities to respond quickly with feedback before moving to independent practice.

- Teach students with cognitive challenges or content area deficits to look to other students for clues before responding (this prevents fear of failure while still promoting engagement).

- Present response slate or whiteboard opportunities while walking around the room rather than always from the front—gain proximity to students who are most likely to struggle with attention to such tasks.

- Because slates have some weight to them, there is the possibility of students inadvertently hitting one another while raising them. Because of this, it is important to teach students the correct and incorrect ways to hold and raise the response slates.

STEP INTO THE FACE-TO-FACE CLASSROOM

Ms. Chu purchases small whiteboards, dry-erase markers, and dry-erase erasers that can be kept on each desk. She explains to the students that after she models and provides guided practice, they will complete several problems on their whiteboard and display them when she says, "Boards up!" The class works through several problems in this manner. Ms. Chu quickly scans the room and makes a note of which students need more practice. During independent practice, she spends individual time with each of these students, reteaching the concept. After class she reflects on the effectiveness of the strategy. She notes the increased engagement of the students and her ability to quickly determine who needs remediation.

CONSIDERATIONS AND DIFFERENTIATION FOR VIRTUAL ENVIRONMENTS

- Consider using response slates or whiteboards only in a synchronous environment, to assess student learning in a quick, efficient manner. This strategy is not compatible with asynchronous learning.

- Because students will need to have the cards outside of the classroom, consider creating a set of laminated cards on a ring that can be delivered to the students' homes.
  - If this is not possible, teach students to make their own response cards and keep them ready for use during each lesson.
  - To make sure that all students have cards for the lesson, ask the students to have them with them for every lesson, or inform them that they will be needed in advance (e.g., included as materials needed for the weekly agenda).

- Consider providing fact sheets or other cues for students with cognitive deficits or students who have difficulty with quick recall.

STEP INTO THE VIRTUAL CLASSROOM

Mr. Steele does not have the ability to purchase or otherwise provide his online students with erasable slates, but he knows that all students have access to clear plastic sheet dividers in their notebooks and dry-erase markers as they were on a list of required materials for the students. He asks the students to put their clear plastic divider on top of white paper and to use their dry-erase markers to diagram sentences. He shows them how to set this up and how to use a dry cloth to erase once they have finished. After diagraming a sentence and clearly describing the rules for how it was diagrammed, Mr. Steele asks the students to write a brief sentence on their divider: "Jacob painted his old house." He then asks them to divide the sentence, one component at a time. "Okay, now that you have it written, I want you to circle the subject and hold it up so that your camera can see it." Once all the students have responded, he provides feedback,

> Everyone did a great job of identifying "Jacob" as the subject. Next, I want you to go back to the sentence and underline the predicate phrase. Remember, you're looking for the part of the sentence that tells us about the subject—what is going on.

The students all go back to work on their sentences for several seconds before Mr. Steele asks, "Okay, let's see what you have. Hold your sentence back up again to show what you have underlined." When he saw students making errors or struggling with a particular component, he explained in detail what the correct response should be and why the alternatives were incorrect.

> Yes, "painted his old house" is the predicate because it tells us what Jacob did. But you would not underline just "old" or just "painted" because that is not the complete statement of what happened.

Mr. Steele used this strategy for the remainder of the diagramming sentences unit and then continued to find ways to get students to write their answers in an erasable format.

ADVANTAGES/DISADVANTAGES

The obvious advantage of the erasable cards and slates is that they provide students with the opportunity to create responses as opposed to selecting from among teacher-provided options. Students can keep the cards or slates at their desks at all times, allowing the teacher to call for a response at any time it is appropriate. In terms of disadvantages, erasable cards and slates can be more difficult to assess as the responses are likely more complex. However, this can be somewhat alleviated by having students respond by group rather than individually. In addition, this strategy requires that students have an erasable writing instrument and eraser—items that are likely to be misplaced.

Hand Signals

Hand signals allow students to use their hands to respond in a number of nonverbal ways. There are several ways to use hand signals to engage students during instruction.

- Fist to five
- Fingers for numbers
- Thumbs up/thumbs down

FIST TO FIVE

STEP INTO THE FACE-TO-FACE CLASSROOM

Ms. Maddow recently learned that student self-assessment can not only lead to increased engagement but also be beneficial for life-long learning. Because of this, she was eager to incorporate this practice into her fifth-grade classroom but was worried that it may be too time-consuming.

STEP INTO THE VIRTUAL CLASSROOM

Ms. Hayes is teaching her seventh-grade health education class online for the first time this year. She is a little nervous that the students will not be as engaged with the online format as they were when she taught a face-to-face class. One thing she wants to do is encourage students to assess their own knowledge before and after a lesson. She thinks that by doing this, students would be more engaged in what they are learning.

The fist-to-five strategy allows students to demonstrate their comfort level, or general level of understanding of the information or concepts that the teacher presents. It is a self-assessment tool that lets students provide a Likert-type rating when prompted by the instructor. When using fist to five, students are able to provide six levels of com-fort or understanding, with

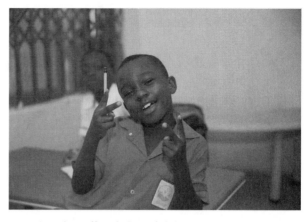

Image source: https://unsplash.com/@k_kyere

the closed fist indicating a 0, or no understanding or comfort, and each raised finger, 1–5, indicating an increasing level of understanding, with 5 signaling the greatest level of comfort or understanding.

BIG IDEA

Students respond to teacher queries about their level of understanding or comfort on new concepts or material by raising a hand that provides a rating of 0–5, with 0 meaning no understanding, indicated by a closed fist. Each progressive level of understanding can be indicated by additional raising of fingers 1 through 5. This self-assessment by students allows the teacher to quickly scan individual students, small groups of students, and even large groups of students in order to assess the general understanding of a concept by all students. This information can then be used by the teacher to determine if a concept needs to be revisited or if additional instruction needs to be provided to individual students, small groups, or the entire class.

Step-by-Step Directions for Use

The fist-to-five strategy can be used in a variety of situations, both planned and unplanned, as long as students have been provided instruction on how the system works, so that they are comfortable in providing a rating when prompted.

(Continued)

(Continued)

1. Teach students how the fist-to-five system works and how you will be using it in your classroom.
   - Explain that they will be rating themselves on their understanding or comfort level on ideas, information, or concepts that you will be discussing in class.
   - A "fist," or level 0, means that you have no understanding or comfort around the information or concept.
   - A "1," or holding one finger in the air, indicates that you understand just a little of what the teacher presented but you are not very comfortable with the information or concept.
   - A "2," or holding two fingers up, indicates that you understand some of what was presented but you still have some information around which you have limited understanding or comfort.
   - A "3," or holding three fingers in the air, indicates that you have a basic understanding of most of what was presented but you did not understand everything, and you still have some room to grow in your understanding or comfort.
   - A "4," or holding four fingers in the air, indicates that you feel pretty comfortable with the concept or information that was presented. Perhaps you did not grasp everything and could still use some help, but in general you feel comfortable with the information and are ready to move on. At this stage the student may just have a few clarifying questions they want to ask.
   - A "5," or holding up all five fingers, indicates that you feel completely comfortable with all of the information presented, you have no clarifying questions, and you are ready for new content or information.

2. Plan to use the fist-to-five strategy during instruction.
   - Determine in what parts of the lesson you will want to gauge the students' level of understanding.
   - Remember, you are trying to engage the students with the lesson and get an accurate idea of their level of understanding, so be sure that the ideas you ask them to rate are the key concepts in the lesson that students need to understand. You are not trying to trick them! You just want to know how they assess their understanding or comfort level.

3. Remind students before the lesson that you will be asking them to use the fist-to-five strategy at different points in the lesson. If you have not used the strategy for a few days, it might be necessary to give a brief refresher on the main points of the strategy.

4. After presenting information during the lesson, ask students to rate their understanding or comfort level on the information using fist to five. Allow a few seconds for students to provide a response. It may be necessary to provide an additional prompt if a few students have not responded. Give positive feedback to students for responding, regardless of the rating they provide. Remember, you are doing this to get their rating so that you can adjust your instruction!

5. Take note of the number of each response that you receive. This information will allow you to provide targeted instruction to those who need it or additional information to the entire group, depending on the responses from the students.

- Consider using a visual aid that depicts the ranking that is not too specific so that it can be used in various contexts.

- Consider helping students calibrate their responses by planned practice activities using the strategy with concepts and information that they already have been exposed to during previous instruction.

- Consider taking time periodically to go back and teach the strategy again. This is particularly helpful to students with disabilities or struggling learners in general.

- Ensure that students are able to provide their responses without other students seeing their response. This helps ensure that students are comfortable in providing accurate responses.

- Be sure to convey to students that it is okay to be at a level 1 or 2, or even a 0, in terms of understanding or comfort. The point is not for everyone to say that they have complete understanding and comfort—the point is to be able to engage students in the lesson at hand and to get an accurate assessment of individual student levels of understanding and comfort so that you can adjust your instruction accordingly.

STEP INTO THE FACE-TO-FACE CLASSROOM

Ms. Maddow thought the fist-to-five strategy would be most effective in promoting student self-assessment in a quick and efficient manner. To prepare for the lesson, Ms. Maddow created the following rating scale to gauge their perception:

- 5: I completely understand (I can teach it to others).
- 4: I mostly understand (I can show it to others).
- 3: I understand pretty well.
- 2: I need more practice.

(Continued)

(Continued)

- 1: I need help.
- 0: I don't understand at all.

After creating the rating scale, Ms. Maddow created a poster to be used as a visual. The visual included pictures of hands making each rating.

At the end of the lesson, Ms. Maddow asked the students to use the fist-to-five method to respond to the statement "What is your level of understanding of today's lesson?" Student responses ranged between 3 and 5, indicating a strong level of understanding. This allowed Ms. Maddow to take note of those students who might need additional support. Overall, Ms. Maddow was pleased with the fist-to-five strategy. She had increased student engagement in the lesson, and she was able to quickly assess student understanding.

Image source: pixabay.com/OpenClipart-Vectors

CONSIDERATIONS AND DIFFERENTIATION FOR VIRTUAL ENVIRONMENTS

- Consider using a visual aid depicting the ranking that is not too specific, so that it can be used in various contexts.

- Consider having students wait for your signal to respond to reduce students being influenced by others.

- Consider tallying responses in real time with a writing instrument and paper, or record the session to go back and review.

- Be sure to convey to students that it is okay to be at level 1 or 2, or even a 0, in terms of understanding or comfort. The point is not for everyone to say they have complete understanding and comfort—the point is to be able to engage students in the lesson at hand and to get an accurate assessment of individual student levels of understanding and comfort so that you can adjust your instruction accordingly.

STEP INTO THE VIRTUAL CLASSROOM

Ms. Hayes decided to use the fist-to-five strategy at the beginning and end of an upcoming lesson on analyzing the components of a nutrition label. To prepare for the lesson, she created the following rating scale to gauge their perception:

- 5: I have complete understanding.
- 4: I mostly understand.
- 3: I understand pretty well.
- 2: I have some understanding.
- 1: I understand very little.
- 0: I don't understand at all.

After creating the rating scale, Ms. Hayes created a visual to be displayed on her computer screen. The visual included pictures of hands making each rating.

(Continued)

(Continued)

To start the lesson, Ms. Hayes displayed the visual and explained to the students,

> Today we are going to talk about the nutrition labels that we see on our food products. Before we get started, I want to see how much you already know. Show me with your hands your level of knowledge about nutrition labels. It can be from a fist, meaning you don't understand at all, to a 5, meaning you have a complete understanding.

Ms. Hayes looked at the grid of students on the computer screen and waited until she saw a response from all the students. She quickly noticed that most of the responses ranged from 1 to 3.

To end the lesson, Ms. Hayes asked her students to self-assess their knowledge again. She displayed the fist-to-five visual on the computer screen and said, "Now that we have learned more about nutrition labels, I want you to show me your level of understanding from fist to five." Ms. Hayes looked at the grid of students and noticed that most of the responses were 3. She replied, "It looks like most students understand pretty well, which is good. We will continue learning more about analyzing nutrition labels in our next class as well."

ADVANTAGES/DISADVANTAGES

There are some obvious advantages in using the fist-to-five strategy. First, there are no materials required. The strategy can be easily employed during essentially any instructional situation. Additionally, the strategy allows teachers to not only increase student engagement with the lesson but also collect assessment data that, in turn, will help inform instruction. Knowing how students assess their own understanding and comfort levels on the content allows the teacher to meet the students where they are functioning. If students need additional instruction or support, the teacher is able to know that and provide what is necessary for them to succeed. In terms of disadvantages, we have to remember that we are asking students to self-assess. This can potentially be problematic because what one student might rate as a "2" in terms of understanding might be rated as a "3" or even a 1" by another student. Calibrating responses across different students can be difficult. It is important that the teacher has a good understanding of different students and how they rate themselves.

FINGERS FOR NUMBERS

STEP INTO THE FACE-TO-FACE CLASSROOM

Ms. David, a middle school social studies teacher, knows that she needs to prepare her students for the upcoming unit exam. She typically displays multiple-choice questions on the interactive whiteboard and asks students to respond, but this has not been effective. The classroom becomes chaotic as some students try to yell the answer out at the same time while others become disengaged. She needs something to get all the students involved, without the opportunity to yell out the answer.

STEP INTO THE VIRTUAL CLASSROOM

Ms. Cassiman is teaching her fifth-grade class online. Although most of the instruction is given asynchronously, where students watch videos and complete assignments on their own time, they meet online as a group for one hour each day. When Ms. Cassiman teaches face-to-face, she enjoys using response cards to actively engage her students, but she is concerned that not all of her students can keep up with them at home.

The fingers-for-numbers strategy allows students to respond to prompts from teachers in a nonverbal way by using their fingers to represent actual numbers as the response. The numbers that students use as responses can correspond to numbered options that have been presented by the teacher, or actual numbers themselves when a question from the teacher requires a response in the form of a number.

Image source: unsplash.com/@hindawi

BIG IDEA

Students respond to teacher queries by holding up a finger to represent a number. This strategy should only be used when the desired response can be given as a number. This could include responses where the answer is provided as a number option. For example, the teacher could have four possible responses on the board and ask students to indicate if the correct answer is number 1, 2, 3, or 4. Or the strategy can be used when the answer is an actual number. For example, the teacher could ask how many seasons are there in one year. In either case the students respond nonverbally by holding up a finger that represents their response.

Step-by-Step Directions for Use

The fingers-for-numbers strategy requires very little setup other than providing instructions to students on how to respond to queries that require a response using a finger as a number. While it can be used in a planned or an unplanned manner, it works best if teachers plan for when the strategy can best be integrated into the instructional plans of each lesson.

1. Teach students the fingers-for-numbers strategy.
   - Teach the specific signal that will be used to occasion the student response.
   - Practice the procedure a few times so that students are comfortable with the procedure.
2. Plan to use fingers for numbers during specific points of instruction.
   - Determine what the questions will be.
   - Make sure that the possible response choices are clear to the students.
   - Make sure that there is a definitive correct answer.
3. Provide reminders to students immediately preceding its use that you are about to use the fingers-for-numbers strategy.
4. After presenting the question, let students know that you are about to provide a signal for them to respond.
   - The signal can simply be the teacher verbally asking the question.
   - Other signals could include a hand motion, a nod, snapping of the fingers, or other physical or gestural prompts.
   - It is important to provide a small amount (i.e., three to five seconds) of wait time between asking the question and signaling for a response. This allows students enough time to process their potential response.

5. After presenting the signal, scan the room for responses.
   - This will allow you to see all who are participating.
   - This also allows you to check for the accuracy of responses.
6. Provide feedback.
   - Provide positive feedback for correct responses.
   - Provide corrective feedback for incorrect responses.

CONSIDERATIONS AND DIFFERENTIATION FOR FACE-TO-FACE ENVIRONMENTS

- Remember to teach the process to students. They must know how they are expected to respond, and they must know the signal that occasions their response.

- To reduce anxiety and students looking at other students' responses, consider having students put their hands in front of their chest.

- Consider pairing students with cognitive deficits, students with disabilities, or struggling learners with a peer who can help with responding.

- Consider having students work in small groups sometimes, and provide them with an opportunity to discuss their response as a group before responding to a query from the teacher.

- Be sure that students are attending before asking the question and providing the signal for a response. The point is not to catch those not attending to the lesson—the point is to increase their engagement in the lesson.

STEP INTO THE FACE-TO-FACE CLASSROOM

Ms. David thought that the fingers-for-numbers strategy would be a great way to prepare her students for the unit exam. Because she already had the review questions created, all she needed to do was put

(Continued)

(Continued)

each multiple-choice question on a digital presentation slide, which she would display on the classroom's interactive whiteboard. The only modification she made was to replace the letters (a, b, c, and d) with numbers (1, 2, 3, and 4).

To begin the review, Ms. David told the class,

> We are going to try something a little different to review what we have learned about the Vietnam War. I am going to display a multiple-choice question and give you 30 seconds to think of an answer. No one is to say a word during this time. Then when I say, "Show me your fingers," you are going to raise the number of fingers of your answer. Okay? Let's try the first question.

Ms. David displayed the question below:

What was the name given to the communist insurgents fighting in South Vietnam?

1. The People's Army of Vietnam

2. The Viet Cong

3. Army of the Republic of Vietnam

4. Khmer Rouge

After 30 seconds, Ms. David gave the students the signal "Show me your fingers" and waited until everyone had an answer. She told them that the correct answer was the Viet Cong. She then continued this process for the rest of the questions.

Ms. David was pleasantly surprised with how this simple strategy allowed all students to participate without the classroom becoming chaotic. Additionally, she was able to quickly assess student learning without calling on individual students.

CONSIDERATIONS AND DIFFERENTIATION FOR VIRTUAL ENVIRONMENTS

- Remember to explicitly teach the signal that you will use to prompt a student response.

- Consider asking follow-up questions immediately after students raise their hand.

  - Ask students to justify or clarify a response, and then call for a revote.

- To prevent students yelling out answers, have students mute their audio so that you will only see their hands.

- To differentiate, have only one student respond with fingers, then ask the others to give a thumbs up/ thumbs down if they agree or not.

STEP INTO THE VIRTUAL CLASSROOM

The students were asked to read a portion of the book *The Borrowers* by Mary Norton, and Ms. Cassiman wanted to give them a few quick comprehension questions to begin the discussion. She thought the fingers-for-numbers strategy would be an effective way to have all students engage in the activity. To prepare, she created multiple-choice comprehension questions on a digital presentation slide, which she would display on her computer screen.

To begin the activity, Ms. Cassiman asked all of her students to mute their computer audio. She then stated,

> As a warm-up, I am going to ask you a few questions about the book we are reading. I am going to show you a multiple-choice question on the screen, and you will have 15 seconds to think of an answer. When you hear the sound of the timer, I want you to show me your answer with your fingers. First question.

Ms. Cassiman displayed the question below on the computer screen and set a visual timer of 15 seconds.

Question 1: How did the little people get the name "The Borrowers"?

1. They borrow things from humans to live.
2. They made it up.
3. It is the name of their house.
4. It is their last name.

When the students heard the sound of the visual timer, they all showed the number one with their fingers in unison. Ms. Cassiman stated, "Yes, they borrow things from humans to live. Great job! Everyone got that answer correct! Let's try a few more."

On reflection, Ms. Cassiman thought that the fingers-for-numbers strategy worked just as well as the response card in engaging all of her students. The activity went so well that she was determined to incorporate the strategy into other content areas as well.

ADVANTAGES/DISADVANTAGES

One major advantage of using fingers for numbers is its simplicity. You do not need any tangible items to employ the strategy. Also, the strategy can be used in a variety of academic content areas. With very little training needed on how to use the strategy, fingers for numbers can be easily used with students across content areas by teachers with any level of experience. One minor disadvantage is that using the strategy does take some planning on the part of the teacher to ensure that instructional material is prepared in a way that allows students to respond with numbers. Obviously, this type of strategy does not work in instances where open-ended responses are expected.

THUMBS UP/THUMBS DOWN

Thumbs up/thumbs down is simply providing students with a means to respond nonverbally to questions or ideas that are presented in class during instruction. Usually, thumbs up/thumbs down signals agreement or disagreement with something stated in class, but it can also convey like or dislike of something, a feeling of good or not good, or even a general understanding or not understanding, depending on the topic being covered in class.

Image source: unsplash.com/JeswinThomas

BIG IDEA

Students respond to queries from the teacher by indicating a thumbs up gesture or a thumbs down gesture. This can be used to indicate agreement or disagreement with a particular statement. For example, the teacher may make a statement about the cause of the Civil War and then ask students if they agree or disagree with the statement by showing a thumbs up or a thumbs down. Additionally, the strategy can be used to indicate if a problem was done correctly or not or if an answer is accurate or not. This use of the strategy could entail the teacher completing a mathematics problem on the board and then asking students if the answer is correct or incorrect, or if the problem was completed using the correct process. Regardless of the type of situation in which the thumbs up/thumbs down strategy is used, it is a simple nonverbal response system that allows the teacher to gauge student knowledge or perceptions about a specific topic.

Step-by-Step Directions for Use

The thumbs up/thumbs down strategy requires very little setup other than providing instructions to students on how to respond to queries that require a response using a thumbs up or a thumbs down. While it can be used in a planned or an unplanned manner, it works best if teachers plan for when the strategy can best be integrated into the instructional plan of each lesson.

1. Teach students the thumbs up/thumbs down strategy.

   - Teach the specific signal that will be used to occasion the student response.

   - Practice the procedure a few times so that students are comfortable with the procedure.

2. Plan to use thumbs up/thumbs down during specific points of instruction.

   - Determine what the questions will be.

   - Make sure that the possible response choices are clear to students.

   - With thumbs up/thumbs down, there does not always need to be a correct answer. In some cases, there may be a correct answer, and students will indicate agreement or disagreement with a specific answer. However, in some cases the student may be indicating how they feel about their level of understanding of a topic, or something similar. In those cases just closely monitor the student responses.

3. Provide reminders to students immediately preceding its use that you are about to use the thumbs up/thumbs down strategy.

4. After presenting the question, let students know that you are about to provide a signal for them to respond.

   - The signal can simply be the teacher verbally asking the question.

   - Other signals could include a hand motion, a nod, snapping of the fingers, or other physical or gestural prompts.

   - It is important to provide a small amount (i.e., three to five seconds) of wait time between asking the question and signaling for a response. This allows students enough time to process their potential response.

5. After presenting the signal, scan the room for responses.

   - This will allow you to see all those participating.

   - This also allows you to check for accuracy of responses or to review responses that are not necessarily correct or incorrect.

6. Provide feedback.

   - Provide positive feedback for correct responses (in cases where there are correct and incorrect responses).

   - Provide corrective feedback for incorrect responses (in cases where there are correct and incorrect responses).

   - In situations where students are responding to indicate if they understand something or if they agree with someone, provide feedback as appropriate based on the student responses.

CONSIDERATIONS AND DIFFERENTIATION FOR FACE-TO-FACE ENVIRONMENTS

- Remember to teach the process to students. They must know how they are expected to respond, and they must know the signal that occasions their response.

- Consider pairing students with cognitive deficits, students with disabilities, or struggling learners with a peer who can help with responding.

- Consider having students discuss their responses in small groups before responding to a query from the teacher.

- Be sure that students are attending before asking the question and providing the signal for a response. The point is not to catch those not attending to the lesson—the point is to increase their engagement in the lesson.

- Be sure to provide feedback to students in a timely manner. If they respond with a correct response, provide positive feedback. If their response is incorrect, provide corrective feedback. Be certain to follow up with additional instruction or information as needed.

STEP INTO THE FACE-TO-FACE CLASSROOM

Mr. Jackson decided to have his students use hand signals to respond to him during the lesson. While teaching a lesson on fractions, Mr. Jackson asked the students to give a thumbs up or thumbs down to the statement "The top number in this fraction is the numerator." He lets the students think for three to five seconds and then scans their responses. All the students had a thumbs up, which indicated the correct answer. Had anyone had a thumbs down, Mr. Jackson would have needed to provide feedback differently to that student than he did for the other students.

CONSIDERATIONS AND DIFFERENTIATION FOR VIRTUAL ENVIRONMENTS

- Consider giving students three choices: (1) thumbs up if you agree, (2) thumbs down if you disagree, and (3) thumbs to the side if you don't know. If concerned about a student always choosing the "I don't know" option, limit their opportunities (e.g., the option can be used only three times per lesson).

- Consider combining with individual questioning strategies (see Section 1), where students are prompted to agree or disagree with an answer by showing a thumbs up or thumbs down.

- Consider asking follow-up questions immediately after students show a thumbs up or a thumbs down.
  - If using as an agree/disagree option, select students to justify their reasoning (e.g., "You disagree. Why?").
  - If using for students to self-assess understanding, select students to explain their answer (e.g., "Is there something specific that is giving you trouble?").

STEP INTO THE VIRTUAL CLASSROOM

Ms. Casey thought using the thumbs up/thumbs down strategy would be an effective, low-risk strategy to increase engagement for all students. Because she is just interested in all students participating, she decided to modify the strategy to include three choices: thumbs up if you agree, thumbs down if you disagree, and thumbs to the side if you don't know.

When reviewing the relationship among latitude, longitude, and temperature in science, Ms. Casey posed the following question to the class: "How is latitude related to temperature?" She then asked for volunteers to raise their hand. She called on a student, who replied, "The farther you get from the equator, the colder it gets." Ms. Casey immediately replied, "Okay class, give me a thumbs up if you agree, a thumbs down if you don't agree, and a thumb to the side if you just don't know." After seeing some students not responding, she said, "I see some students are still deciding. We will wait until everyone has made their decision." After everyone had their thumbs up, Ms. Casey continued, "If you had your thumbs up, you are correct! The relationship between latitude and temperature involves temperatures typically being warmer when approaching the equator and cooler when approaching the poles."

Ms. Casey paid particular attention to the few students who were usually reluctant to participate. She could see that they were still a little hesitant to answer and may have been copying other students' responses, but that was okay. This was just an attempt to build their confidence in participating with a low-risk request.

ADVANTAGES/DISADVANTAGES

The thumbs up/thumbs down strategy has numerous advantages. First, it is a simple strategy that can be used in a variety of situations. It can be used to indicate agreement if something is correct or not correct, or even to let the teacher know if the student understands the topic at hand. In addition, it is a strategy that students have usually used as part of their normal communication techniques for most of their lives. The thumbs up/thumbs down signal is generally a universal form of communication that can be used in a variety of settings and situations, and it does not require any tangible items to employ it. It can be used within essentially any content area and at any age level of student. However, the strategy is not effective when a more in-depth student response is required, including open-ended responses, or when students are required to verbalize a specific response.

SECTION 3

Partner and Team Engagement Strategies

Partner and team responses involve students working together to formulate a response and can incorporate both verbal and nonverbal responding. Responses for these strategies range from very quick one-word answers to longer discussions. There are six key ways in which partner and team engagement strategies can be used.

1. Turn and talk
2. Cued retell
3. Numbered heads together
4. Four corners
5. Snowball
6. Classroom mingle

Partner and team engagement strategies can be logistically cumbersome for teachers to implement with ease and efficiency in an online environment. Implementation is dependent on the features provided by the software being used and the technological knowledge of the teacher. For this reason implementing partner and team engagement strategies in the virtual environment will not be included.

Turn and Talk

STEP INTO THE CLASSROOM

Mr. Raney is a high school civics teacher looking for ways to increase engagement in his instruction. His primary OTR strategy during instruction has been to offer a question to the whole class and select students who volunteer to respond by raising their hand. However, he finds it is the same few students volunteering while others seem to "check out" of the lesson. He is specifically looking for a strategy that is quick and easy to implement and will allow for all students to engage in more in-depth discussions.

Turn and talk, also known as think-pair-share, is a strategy that allows students to have a purposeful discussion with a partner on a specific topic. Discussion prompts can include sharing prior knowledge of a topic, fostering in-depth discussion of content that was just presented, or generating new ideas.

BIG IDEA

By having students discuss a question or prompt about a topic or assigned reading with a partner, this strategy gives all students the opportunity to actively participate in the discussion rather than calling on volunteers in large-group discussions. Additionally, students may feel more comfortable discussing topics with a partner rather than in a large-group setting. This strategy is useful across all grade levels and content areas.

Step-by-Step Directions for Use

Turn and talk requires minimal teacher preparation. Although this strategy can be used in both a planned and an unplanned manner, preplanning the questions/prompts to be given to students is suggested. Questions/prompts can be delivered before, during, and after the lesson. There are no resources needed for the student to participate in this activity.

1. Strategically assign students to partners.
   - Partners can be assigned in various ways, but we suggest purposefully assigning students, such as in heterogeneous groupings (e.g., low-performing student with middle-performing student), rather than allowing students to decide or selecting at random.
   - Sit partners together, and assign each student with a designation (e.g., 1, 2; A, B).

2. Stop at a predetermined time in the lesson, and introduce the turn-and-talk procedure.
   - Initially, explicitly teach and model the step-by-step process as well as expectations such as how to work with peers appropriately.
   - As students become familiar with the process, briefly review procedures and expectations.

3. Present students with a prompt/question.
   - Questions at the beginning of a lesson could be used to activate prior knowledge or to review prerequisite skills.
   - Questions/prompts during the lesson could be used for students to have a more in-depth conversation on a specific topic, generate ideas or opinions, and clarify misconceptions.
   - Questions/prompts after the lesson could be used to review critical aspects of the content learned, make connections to content previously learned, and provide relevance to the content learned.

4. Give students adequate time to think of a response to the question or prompt.
   - Length of time will depend on the question/prompt given and the age of students.
   - Provide clear and consistent cues for how much time is available. This can include using a visual timer or verbally stating increments of time (e.g., "You have one more minute to finish your thought").

5. Prompt students to begin discussing the question or prompt.
   - Length of time will depend on the question/prompt given and the age of students.
   - Provide clear and consistent cues for how much time is available. This can include using a visual timer or verbally stating increments of time (e.g., "You have one more minute to wrap up your discussion").

(Continued)

(Continued)

6. Monitor student discussions, and provide assistance when needed.

7. Have students share their responses to the question/prompt by asking for volunteers, selecting specific students to model correct responses, or randomly selecting students.

8. Provide specific feedback related to both the content of their responses and their participation in the stop-and-jot procedure.

CONSIDERATIONS AND DIFFERENTIATION FOR FACE-TO-FACE ENVIRONMENTS

- Consider using questions and prompts with simple answers when students are initially learning the turn-and-talk strategy, and gradually increase the complexity as they become more comfortable with the routine.

- Consider explicitly teaching students how to be effective listeners and speakers. This may include instruction on turn taking, speaking clearly, and providing appropriate feedback.

- Consider using visuals such as anchor charts to initially teach the strategy and later as a reminder for students.

- Consider combining with the stop-and-jot strategy (see Section 2), where students will share their written responses with a partner before sharing with the class.

- Provide assistance to students who have difficulties with processing information.

STEP INTO THE CLASSROOM

Mr. Raney decided to use the turn-and-talk strategy when planning an upcoming lesson on why voting is an important responsibility for young citizens. When creating his presentation slides, he included slides with questions that prompted more in-depth discussion at the beginning, during, and end of the lesson. The slide header was titled "Turn and Talk," and the content displayed the prompt and the amount of time for discussion. This would serve as a prompt for him and a support for the students. Additionally, he looked over his class roster and strategically assigned students in heterogeneous groupings. He listed the partners on a presentation slide, with each partner having a determination of either a "1" or a "2."

At the beginning of the lesson Mr. Raney told the students that there will be times when he will ask them to turn to a partner and discuss. He then showed the students the presentation slide that listed the partners and said, "Before we begin, I want you to find your partner on this list and sit by them for the remainder of this lesson." Once the students were sitting next to their partners, Mr. Raney asked them to remember if they were a "1" or a "2."

At the first turn-and-talk opportunity Mr. Raney brought the students' attention to the "Turn and Talk" slide and said, "This is our first time to turn and talk. First, I want you to take two minutes to think about the following question to yourself: What can be done to get younger people out to vote?" After the students were given time to think, Mr. Raney then said,

> Now I want you to turn to your partner and discuss what can be done to get younger people out to vote. You will have two minutes to talk, and then I will ask either the 1s or the 2s to share what they have discussed.

As the students were talking, Mr. Raney circulated the classroom and provided assistance to those students who needed it. Once the time was up, he asked the 1s from each pair to tell the whole class what was discussed. He used the same process for the other two turn-and-talk opportunities he had planned for the lesson.

Mr. Raney was very happy with the results of the turn-and-talk strategy. Not only was it very easy to implement, but all the students were also able to actively engage in the lesson. In fact, he noticed that students who typically were reluctant to participate in whole-group discussions were sharing responses with their partner. He was determined to implement this strategy on a regular basis so that it would become a part of the classroom routine.

ADVANTAGES/DISADVANTAGES

The turn-and-talk strategy gives all students the opportunity to actively participate in the discussion. Additionally, asking students to discuss what they are learning in a more in-depth manner promotes greater comprehension of the content as well as allowing the teacher to formatively assess student learning. Furthermore, students who may be reluctant to participate in large-group discussions may feel more comfortable participating with a partner. The one disadvantage of this strategy is that the more extroverted students may dominate the discussion, while the more introverted students may be passively engaged. Additionally, in a larger setting the teacher may not be able to monitor all students to ensure that they are remaining on task.

Cued Retell

Cued retell is a strategy that allows students to work in pairs to "retell" concepts or terms they have just read or have been learning. This strategy is generally used for reviewing concepts that were recently taught or as a post-reading comprehension activity.

Image source: https://unsplash.com/@mimithian

BIG IDEA

Working in pairs, one partner will try to recall everything they can about a concept, terms from a passage, or the steps in a process, while the other partner listens and provides prompting/support when necessary. This provides students additional opportunities to review previously learned or read material as well as practice skills such as active listening and speaking. This strategy is useful across all grade levels and content areas.

Step-by-Step Directions for Use

Cued retell requires minimal teacher preparation. Preplanning the prompts to be given and creating the cued retell topic sheet, which includes the information to be recalled, will be needed. Students will need a copy of the cued retell topic sheet and a writing instrument.

(Continued)

(Continued)

1. Strategically assign students to partners.

   - Partners can be assigned in various ways, but we suggest purposefully assigning students, such as in heterogeneous groupings (e.g., low-performing student with middle-performing student), rather than allowing students to decide or selecting at random.

   - Sit partners together, and assign each student with a designation (e.g., 1, 2; A, B).

2. Stop at a predetermined time in the lesson, and introduce the cued retell procedure.

   - Initially, explicitly teach and model the step-by-step process as well as expectations such as how to work with peers appropriately.

   - As students become familiar with the process, briefly review the procedures and expectations.

3. Present students with the prompt, and hand out the cued retell topic sheet.

   - Prompts at the beginning of a lesson could be used to review previously learned materials or prerequisite skills.

   - Prompts during the lesson could be used to review important details or facts being presented in the lesson.

   - Prompts after the lesson could be used to review critical aspects of the content learned.

4. Prompt students to begin the cued retell procedure.

   - Partner 1 will begin by retelling everything they can about concepts or terms just read or the steps in a process.

   - Using the cued retell sheet, partner 2 will check off the items that are recalled by partner 1 under the column "Independent."

   - If partner 1 does not remember the items, partner 2 will offer cues to assist with recalling the information.

   - Using the cued retell sheet, partner 2 will check off items that are recalled after prompting under the column "Cues."

5. The partners switch roles.

6. Monitor the students, and provide specific feedback related to both the content of their responses and their participation in the cued retell procedure.

CONSIDERATIONS AND DIFFERENTIATION FOR FACE-TO-FACE ENVIRONMENTS

- When switching roles, consider giving students different prompts or reading passages to retell.

- Consider explicitly teaching students how to be effective listeners and speakers. This may include instruction on how to cue without giving away the answer and providing appropriate feedback.

- Consider providing students with a list of possible cues (e.g., "What about _____?")

- Consider using this strategy for nonacademic processes such as social skills instruction.

- Ensure that students are able to read all the items on the cued retell sheet.

STEP INTO THE CLASSROOM

Ms. Noble decided to use the cued retell strategy to help students review the steps of the scientific method. To prepare for the review, she created a cued retell sheet that included the following information:

STEPS OF THE SCIENTIFIC METHOD	INDEPENDENT	CUES
1. Make an observation.		
2. Ask a question about the observation, and gather information.		
3. Form a hypothesis, or testable explanation.		
4. Test the hypothesis.		
5. Analyze the data, and draw conclusions; accept or reject the hypothesis, or modify the hypothesis if necessary		

Additionally, she looked over her class roster and strategically assigned students into homogeneous groupings.

At the beginning of the activity, Ms. Noble explained to the students that they were going to work with a partner to help review the steps of the scientific method. After the students were told who their partner was, she stated, "I want you to get with your partner and show me with your fingers if you are a 1 or a 2." As she handed out the cued retell sheet to the students holding up the number 2, Ms. Noble stated,

Okay, I want the 1s to tell the 2s the steps of the scientific method. If you get stuck, it's okay. The 2s will help you by using

(*Continued*)

(Continued)

their cued retell sheet. And 2s, if the 1s get the step correct the first time, mark "Independent" on your sheet; if they need a cue from you, mark "Cue" on your sheet. After all the information has been covered, share the results and discuss.

After the students had discussed the results with their partner, they were prompted to switch roles and repeat the process.

As the students were completing the activity, Ms. Noble moved around the classroom to observe and answer questions. This strategy seemed to be more effective than her whole-group review. Not only were all the students actively engaged, but the results of the cued retell sheet also allowed her to assess student progress.

ADVANTAGES/DISADVANTAGES

The cued retell strategy keeps all students actively involved in the learning process, whether they have the role of telling or cueing. It is an effective and time-efficient strategy to practice or review concepts, terms, or the steps in a process, and it also allows the teacher to formatively assess student learning. Furthermore, students who may not be confident answering questions or giving feedback in large-group activities may feel more comfortable doing so when they have the aid of the cued retell sheet. The main disadvantage of this strategy is that you are limited to tasks that require list-like answers; therefore, it is typically used for practice and review. Additionally, because this strategy is dependent on students being able to read the cue sheet, it may not be suitable for younger students and for older students who are reading significantly below grade level.

Numbered Heads Together

STEP INTO THE CLASSROOM

Mr. Sanchez, a first-year special education teacher in a self-contained classroom for students with emotional disorders, was having difficulty with managing behavior during his mathematics lessons. He thought that he was doing a good job of delivering the content, but he noticed that the same few students were actively participating, while the rest of the students were disengaged and causing disruptions, preventing others from learning. He was looking for an activity that would increase engagement while also giving his students opportunities to practice working with others.

Numbered heads together (NHT; Kagan, 1992) is a cooperative learning strategy where students work together in teams to answer a question or problem. Questions include, but are not limited to, answering comprehension questions or mathematics problems, evaluating a passage or a piece of writing, and reviewing previously learned content.

BIG IDEA

Students are placed in teams, and each student in the team is given a number. After the teams "put their heads together" to answer a question or problem, the teacher randomly selects a student from the team to share their answer. This random selection holds each student accountable for knowing and sharing the answer to a question or problem. This strategy is useful across all grade levels and content areas.

Step-by-Step Directions for Use

NHT requires teacher preparation. Preplanning the questions or problems that will be given to students is needed. Students will need a writing instrument (e.g., pencil, pen, dry-erase marker) and writing surface (e.g., paper, response slate).

1. Strategically assign students to teams.
   - Teams can be assigned in various ways, but we suggest purposefully assigning students, such as in heterogeneous groupings (e.g., a mix of low-performing, average-performing, and high-performing students), rather than allowing students to decide or selecting at random.
   - Sit teams together, and assign each student within the team a number (e.g., 1, 2, 3, 4).

2. Stop at a predetermined time in the lesson, and introduce NHT.
   - Initially, explicitly teach and model the step-by-step process as well as expectations such as how to work with peers appropriately.
   - As students become familiar with the process, briefly review the procedures and expectations.

3. Present students with the question or problem, and prompt them to independently write their answer to the problem.
   - Length of time will depend on the question/problem given and the age of students.
   - Provide clear and consistent cues for how much time is available. This can include using a visual timer or verbally stating increments of time (e.g., "You have one more minute to finish writing your response").

4. Have students "put their heads together" to discuss their individual answers and come to a consensus on the team's final answer.
   - Length of time will depend on the question/problem given and the age of students.
   - Provide clear and consistent cues for how much time is available. This can include using a visual timer or verbally stating increments of time (e.g., "You have one more minute to come to a consensus").

5. Randomly call out a number, and prompt students with that number to share their teams' answer.

6. Monitor the students, and provide specific feedback related to both the content of their responses and their participation in the NHT procedure.

CONSIDERATIONS AND DIFFERENTIATION FOR FACE-TO-FACE ENVIRONMENTS

- Consider providing fewer, simpler questions or problems for younger students, which may include drawing pictures or symbols instead of writing.

- Consider combining with the hand signals strategy (see Section 2), where students are prompted to agree or disagree with an answer by showing thumbs up or thumbs down.

- After one student gives the group's answer, consider selecting another student from the team to explain or justify the group's reasoning.

- To save paper, consider having students write their answers on response slates.

- Consider explicitly teaching students how to interact with others in a group. This may include instruction on turn taking, speaking clearly, and providing appropriate feedback.

- Consider grouping numbers by ability (e.g., all 1s are high performing, all 2s and 3s are average, and all 4s are low performing) to allow you to differentiate the questions being asked or the problems being given.

STEP INTO THE CLASSROOM

Mr. Sanchez decided to incorporate NHT into a review on area and circumference of a circle. Prior to the lesson, he strategically assigned students into three heterogeneous groups of four and created 10 problems for the students to answer.

At the beginning of class Mr. Sanchez told the students that they were going to work in groups to answer questions on area and circumference of a circle. He then stated, "Now, for this to work, we are going to have to work together with our partners. This will include making sure everyone gets a turn to speak, using appropriate language, and being supportive of one another." When putting students in their groups, Mr. Sanchez handed each group a dry-erase board and asked each person in the group to count off 1–4. He then explained to the class,

> It is important that everyone puts their "heads together" to come up with the answer because I will be randomly choosing a number from 1 to 4. The student who represents this number will give your groups' answer to the rest of the class. You will

(Continued)

have three minutes to answer the problem. Everyone ready? The first problem is to find the area of a circle with a radius of 10 inches.

As Mr. Sanchez circulated the room, he noticed that all the students were actively engaged in answering the problem. After three minutes, he called "time" and randomly called out a number for each group and had those students represent their group's answer. After each group had had a chance to respond, he repeated the process for the remaining nine problems.

Overall, Mr. Sanchez was pleased with the effectiveness of the strategy. He witnessed students representing their groups who had rarely participated before. These students seemed more at ease now because they had the group's written response to use as a guide. He was also able to ask follow-up questions to other members of the group in an attempt to clarify or justify a response. Because of the success of this lesson, Mr. Sanchez planned to incorporate this strategy into future lessons.

ADVANTAGES/DISADVANTAGES

The NHT strategy keeps all students involved in the learning process by holding each student accountable for knowing the answer to a question or problem. Students become responsible not only for their own learning but for that of others as well. Additionally, the use of NHT has been associated with improvement in both academic performance and on-task behavior for students with disabilities in inclusive and self-contained settings (Haydon, Maheady, et al., 2010; Hunter & Haydon, 2013; Maheady et al., 1991; Maheady et al., 2006). The one disadvantage of this strategy is that the more extroverted students may dominate the discussion, while the more introverted students may be passively engaged. Similarly, there is a risk that students may just copy the answer of another student. If the teacher cannot prevent this from happening, other strategies mentioned in this book may be more effective.

Four Corners

STEP INTO THE CLASSROOM

Ms. Donan is a third-grade teacher planning an upcoming unit on persuasive writing. In the past, she would introduce a topic to the students and then model how to write a persuasive essay on the topic. Although this seemed to work well for most students, not all students were engaged in the lesson. She was looking for a strategy to introduce persuasive writing that would engage all students.

Four corners is a cooperative learning strategy where students are asked to make a decision about a question, problem, or statement. Students are typically presented with a controversial statement or problem, but it could also be used for multiple-choice question types.

BIG IDEA

The four-corners strategy asks students to move to a corner of the classroom that best represents their response. Once in their corner, students will discuss their idea with others in their corner, and the teacher will randomly select a student to summarize their ideas to the class. This strategy promotes active listening, critical thinking, and decision-making and is useful across all grade levels and content areas.

Step-by-Step Directions for Use

The four-corners strategy requires teacher preparation. Preplanning the questions or problems that will be given to students and creating the posters representing responses will be needed. For older students it is suggested to have chart paper and writing tools at each corner to aid in summarizing their response.

(Continued)

(Continued)

1. Stop at a predetermined time in the lesson, and introduce the four-corners strategy.

   - Present students with the four different responses, and place them in four different areas of the classroom.

   - Responses could include, but are not limited to, the following: Strongly agree, Agree, Disagree, and Strongly disagree, or A, B, C, and D.

2. Present students with the question, problem, or statement, and prompt them to independently think about their response.

   - Length of time will depend on the question/problem given and the age of students.

   - Provide clear and consistent cues for how much time is available. This can include using a visual timer or verbally stating increments of time (e.g., "You have one more minute to think about your response").

3. Ask students to move to the corner that best represents their response.

   - Length of time will depend on the question/problem given and the age of students.

   - Provide clear and consistent cues for how much time is available. This can include using a visual timer or verbally stating increments of time (e.g., "You have one more minute to select a corner").

4. Prompt students to discuss their reasons for selecting this response.

   - Length of time will depend on the question/problem given and the age of students.

   - Provide clear and consistent cues for how much time is available. This can include using a visual timer or verbally stating increments of time (e.g., "You have one more minute to summarize your ideas").

   - For older students designate a person in the group to summarize responses on chart paper.

5. Randomly select a student to share their team's answer.

6. Monitor the students, and provide specific feedback related to both the content of their responses and their participation in the four-corners procedure.

CONSIDERATIONS AND DIFFERENTIATION FOR FACE-TO-FACE ENVIRONMENTS

- Consider initially providing fewer response types for younger students (e.g., yes/no; agree/disagree), then gradually increase them as they become proficient with the process.

- Consider giving each student in the group a responsibility for facilitating discussion (e.g., facilitator, recorder, summarizer, timekeeper).

- Consider having students use sticky notes to write down their response during independent think time and placing them on the chart paper to facilitate the group discussion.

- After one student gives the group's response, consider asking other students in the group follow-up questions to expand on the response.

- Once each group has shared responses, consider asking the students if they would change their response.

- To save paper, consider having students write answers on response slates.

STEP INTO THE CLASSROOM

Ms. Donan decided to use the four-corners strategy to introduce her students to persuasive writing. To prepare for the lesson, she needed to think of a statement that not only would allow for students to have different viewpoints but also would be interesting. She decided on the statement "Animals should be kept in the zoo." She then used poster boards to create four signs. For each sign she wrote the following in large letters: Strongly agree, Agree, Disagree, and Strongly disagree. Finally, she placed each of the posters in four separate corners of the classroom.

To begin the activity, Ms. Donan explained to the students that they will be learning about persuasive essays in writing for the next few weeks and that she has a fun activity called four corners that will help them get started. She then read the statement out loud to the class and asked them to quietly think about it for three minutes. After the time had elapsed, she stated,

> Okay, now that you have had some time to think about it, I want you to get up and move to the poster that best represents how you feel (pointing to each poster). Do you strongly agree, agree, disagree, or strongly disagree with the statement? Remember, there are no right or wrong answers.

Ms. Donan allowed a few minutes for the students to transition to their corners and assisted those students who were having difficulty with their decision.

(Continued)

(Continued)

Once all the students had made their decision, Ms. Donan asked each group to discuss their reasoning for choosing this opinion. She then selected a note taker for each group to record the group's responses and reminded them that she will randomly select a representative from each group to share the group's response. Ms. Donan set a timer for five minutes and circulated the classroom to assist and provide feedback where necessary. Finally, she selected a student from each group to share their reasons with the whole group.

Reflecting on the activity, Ms. Donan thought that the four-corners strategy allowed her to introduce persuasive writing in a fun and engaging way. Students were actively engaged by getting out of their seats and discussing their opinions with other students. She also decided to leave the posters up in the classroom to use throughout the school year.

ADVANTAGES/DISADVANTAGES

The four-corners strategy promotes active engagement through movement and discussion. Additionally, students will learn from others as they build on one another's ideas as well as learn to hear differing viewpoints from the other groups. Although it is generally used for having students critically think about controversial statements, opinions, or problems, it can also be used as a review for a quiz or test by using multiple choice question types. The main disadvantage of this strategy is the potential for disruptions while transitioning to responses. Some students may choose to go to the same area as their friend(s) or not choose an area in a timely manner. If the teacher cannot prevent this from happening, using one of the response card strategies mentioned in this book may be more effective.

Snowball

The snowball strategy allows students to discuss a topic in greater depth by gradually increasing the number of students sharing information. This strategy is best used for open-ended discussions that allow students to build on one another's responses.

Image source: https://unsplash.com/@cdc

BIG IDEA

The snowball strategy asks students to first reply to a question or prompt individually, then discuss in pairs, then in groups of four, and so on. It allows for students to independently formulate their own ideas on a topic and then gradually synthesize them with other information.

This provides students additional opportunities to learn new material and practice skills such as active listening and speaking, as well as allowing the teacher to assess student learning. This strategy is most useful with older students and with content that allows for several sequenced, open-ended questions or tasks rather than discrete questions with answers that are right or wrong.

Step-by-Step Directions for Use

The snowball strategy requires minimal teacher preparation. Preplanning the questions/tasks to be given to students will be needed. Questions/tasks can be delivered before, during, and after the lesson. Students will need a writing instrument (e.g., pencil, pen, dry-erase marker) and writing surface (e.g., paper, response slate, stop-and-jot graphic organizer).

1. Stop at a predetermined time in the lesson, and introduce the snowball strategy.
   - Initially, explicitly teach and model the step-by-step process as well as expectations such as how to work with peers appropriately.
   - As students become familiar with the process, briefly review the procedures and expectations.
2. Present students with a question or task, and ask them to independently write a response.
3. Give students adequate time to write a response to the question or prompt.
   - Length of time will depend on the prompt/task given.
   - Provide clear and consistent cues for how much time is available. This can include using a visual timer or verbally stating increments of time (e.g., "You have one more minute to finish writing your response").
4. Prompt students to begin discussing the question or task with a partner, and give adequate time for discussion.
   - The teacher can strategically assign partners or allow students to choose.
   - Length of time will depend on the prompt/task given.
5. Combine pairs into groups of four, ask the groups to begin discussing the question or task, and give adequate time for discussion.
   - Can be the same question/task, or a new question/task can be introduced.
   - Can strategically combine groups or allow students to choose.
   - Length of time will depend on the question/prompt given.
6. Continue combining groups until it becomes a whole-class discussion.
   - Can be the same question/task, or a new question/task can be introduced.
7. Monitor the students, and provide specific feedback related to both the content of their responses and their participation in the snowball procedures.

CONSIDERATIONS AND DIFFERENTIATION FOR FACE-TO-FACE ENVIRONMENTS

- Consider stopping the snowball activity after groups of four and having representatives from each group share their group's discussion.

- Consider explicitly teaching students how to be effective listeners and speakers. This may include instruction on turn taking, speaking clearly, and providing appropriate feedback.

- As groups get larger, consider giving each student in the group a responsibility for facilitating discussion (e.g., facilitator, recorder, summarizer, timekeeper).

- Consider using this strategy for nonacademic processes such as social skills instruction.

STEP INTO THE CLASSROOM

Ms. Dieng was planning to show a short film during an upcoming lesson on the American civil rights movement. She decided to use the snowball activity to foster an in-depth discussion of the video. To prepare for the activity, Ms. Dieng created a graphic organizer that students would be given to complete during the film, which would help facilitate the discussion afterward. The graphic organizer prompted the students to do the following: (1) list three things you did not know about the American civil rights movement before watching the film, (2) list two questions you still have after watching the film, and (3) describe the most memorable moment from the film.

When introducing the film, Ms. Dieng distributed the graphic organizer and reviewed the prompts that she wanted the students to answer. She stated,

> Your responses don't have to be that long, only a sentence or two. And you don't need to worry about correct spelling or grammar. I just want you to get your thoughts down on paper. And if you don't want to complete while watching, that's okay too. I will give a little time after to work on it.

After the film, Ms. Dieng gave the students five minutes to complete their graphic organizer independently. She then explained,

> Today we are going to do something a little different called the snowball strategy. To start, when I say "Go," I want you to find a partner and discuss the three things you did not know before watching the film. Once everyone has found a partner, I will put three minutes on the timer. Ready, go.

As the students were sharing their thoughts, Ms. Dieng circulated the room and provided feedback.

(Continued)

(Continued)

After three minutes, Ms. Dieng asked each of the student pairs to join another student pair to make a group of four. Once in their groups, she explained, "I want you to discuss the three things you did not know before watching the film and also share the two questions you still have. I will put five minutes on the timer. Ready, go." As the students were sharing their thoughts, Ms. Dieng circulated the room and provided feedback. After five minutes, she asked each group to join another group to make groups of eight. The students were given three minutes to describe their most memorable moment from the film. At the conclusion of the activity Ms. Dieng asked for volunteers to share what they had learned to the whole group.

Overall, Ms. Dieng thought the activity was more effective in engaging all of her students to discuss the film than what she had been previously doing. She saw students building on one another's ideas as the groups gradually got larger. And most important, students who were usually reluctant to participate in the whole-group discussion were sharing their responses in the smaller groups.

ADVANTAGES/DISADVANTAGES

The snowball strategy promotes active engagement through movement and discussion. Students building on one another's ideas to expand their knowledge on a specific topic promotes greater comprehension of the content as well as allowing the teacher to formatively assess student learning. Furthermore, students who may be reluctant to participate in large-group discussions may feel more comfortable participating in this activity. The one disadvantage of this strategy is that the more extroverted students may dominate the discussion while the more introverted students may be passively engaged. Additionally, this activity takes longer than other strategies, which may lead to some students becoming disengaged. If the teacher cannot prevent this from happening, using one of the other strategies mentioned in this book may be more effective.

Classroom Mingle

Classroom mingle, also called mix and mingle, allows students to work in multiple pairs to discuss a topic in greater depth. This strategy can be used to activate prior knowledge, to assess prerequisite skills, or as a review.

BIG IDEA

Classroom mingle allows students to move around the classroom and ask and answer questions with multiple partners. This provides students additional opportunities to learn new material and practice skills such as active listening and speaking, as well as allowing the teacher to assess student learning. This strategy is useful across all grade levels and content areas.

Step-by-Step Directions for Use

Classroom mingle requires minimal teacher preparation. Slips of paper with various questions, statements, or problems will be needed. There are no resources needed for the student to participate in this activity.

(Continued)

(Continued)

1. Stop at a predetermined time in the lesson, and introduce the classroom mingle strategy.
   - Initially, explicitly teach and model the step-by-step process as well as expectations such as how to work with peers appropriately.
   - As students become familiar with the process, briefly review the procedures and expectations.

2. Give each student a slip of paper that has a question or problem, and prompt them to start walking around the classroom until you tell them to stop.

3. Prompt students to stop walking and find a partner who is closest to them.

4. Once in pairs, the students will take turns asking and answering the questions on their slips of paper.
   - Length of time will depend on the question/problem given and the age of students.
   - Provide clear and consistent cues for how much time is available. This can include using a visual timer or verbally stating increments of time (e.g., "You have one more minute").

5. After a set amount of time, the teacher will ask students to trade questions or problems and find another partner.

6. This process will be repeated for a predetermined amount of time or when all the students have shared with a new partner.

7. Monitor the students, and provide specific feedback related to both the content of their responses and their participation in the classroom mingle procedure.

CONSIDERATIONS AND DIFFERENTIATION FOR FACE-TO-FACE ENVIRONMENTS

- For problems that have a right or wrong answer, consider having the answer written on the opposite side of the slip of paper. This will allow students to praise others for a correct answer and provide immediate error correction for wrong answers.

- If more structure is needed, consider asking each pair of students the same question. After discussing, the students will find a new partner, and a new question will be asked.

- Consider having students raise their hand when they have finished answering and asking questions and pair up with another student who has their hand raised.

- After the activity is completed, consider having a whole-group discussion.

- Consider using this strategy for nonacademic processes such as social skills instruction.

- Ensure that students are able to read the question or problem written on the slip of paper.

STEP INTO THE CLASSROOM

Ms. Turner decided to use the classroom mingle strategy to help review fact and opinion. To prepare for the activity, she wrote statements on the front of index cards and identified them as either fact or opinion on the back of the index card. For example, she wrote, "Apples grow on trees" on the front of one card and then "Fact" on the back, while another card said, "Apples taste great" on the front and "Opinion" on the back. In total, she prepared 30 cards (15 facts and 15 opinions).

Because this was the first time the students would be doing this activity, Ms. Turner thought it might be best to model it before asking them to do it independently. Ms. Turner explained,

> In a few minutes I will be giving each of you a card that has a statement on the front and then whether the statement is a fact or an opinion on the back. When I give the signal "Mingle," you are going to find a partner.

She then selected a student to help model the activity and said, "After I find my partner, I am going to show them the front of the card but not the back. They are then going to read the statement and tell me if it is a fact or an opinion." Ms. Turner prompted the student to read the card aloud and then tell her whether it was a fact or an opinion. The student replied, "Fish are ugly. That is an opinion." Ms. Turner let her know the answer was correct and then stated,

> Now she is going to show me the front of her card, and I am going to read it aloud and say whether it is a fact or an opinion. Okay, the card says soccer is played with a ball. That is a fact.

After the student acknowledged that the response was correct, Ms. Turner continued, "After we both have our turn, we will exchange

(Continued)

(Continued)

cards and find a new partner. You will keep doing this until I tell you to stop."

Ms. Turner handed each student a fact or an opinion card and reminded them of the importance of not showing the other student the back of the card. She then had students stand up and gave the signal "Mingle." As the students were doing the activity, Ms. Turner circulated the room to provide assistance where needed. She allowed the activity to continue until each student had read and responded to at least five statements.

ADVANTAGES/DISADVANTAGES

Classroom mingle is a flexible strategy that promotes active engagement through movement and discussion with multiple peers. It provides students with a method to communicate their knowledge and thought process while also being able to learn from others, both of which build on their understanding of a topic. Additionally, it provides teachers with an opportunity to formatively assess learning and provide immediate feedback. However, there are some disadvantages to this strategy. First, pairs are chosen at random (i.e., whoever is closest at the time of the prompt to stop), which eliminates the teacher's ability to strategically pair students together. Additionally, as with any activity that involves movement, there is a greater potential for disruptive behavior during this activity. If the teacher cannot prevent this from happening, using one of the response card strategies mentioned in this book may be more effective.

Conclusion
Putting It All Together

This book has provided you with a range of specific strategies for actively engaging students during instruction. While having knowledge of these strategies is important, it is just the first step. As you may recall, engagement is not done in addition to instruction; it is an inherent component of instruction. As such, OTRs should be planned as part of the lesson and provided at a rate optimal to maintaining student engagement (i.e., an average of three per minute). An action plan may be needed to help support you in starting this endeavor.

IDENTIFYING INSTRUCTIONAL TIMES

Although the goal is to increase active engagement for all instruction, it may be too overwhelming to tackle this all at once. This may lead to frustration and eventually giving up.

For this reason we suggest starting out with identifying the instructional times when student engagement is low and/or disruptive behavior is high. For example, a ninth-grade teacher may identify his first-period social studies class as an area to target due to having a number of his students falling asleep during lectures. On the other hand, a third-grade teacher may identify the afternoon mathematics class as an area to target due to spending too much of her time focused on disciplining off-task behavior rather than instruction.

A quick observation of the daily schedule to identify when students are least likely to be engaged may be appropriate for most teachers, but some may need a more structured approach, especially if they feel like there is more than just one instructional time that needs attention. In this case, you may want to consider using a scatterplot (Touchette et al., 1985) to identify the most problematic classes. To create a scatterplot, you must first break up the school day by the activity (e.g., first period, geometry, reading). Next, you must indicate when off-task or targeted behaviors occur by filling in the boxes associated with the activity and day. This could be done by tallying each time the behavior occurs or indicating levels of behavior. Figure 2 shows an example of a ninth-grade teacher's scatterplot that is broken into periods and identifies levels of participation. From this scatterplot it would seem that the first period would be the class to initially target.

FIGURE 2 ● Classroom scatterplot example

Dates: 9/16–9/20 **Grade:** ninth

Observer: Ms. Stebbins

Target Behaviors: student participation: students speaking

Legend: □ No students speaking   ☒ 1–3 students speaking
■ 4–6 students speaking   ☑ 7+ students speaking

TIME/ACTIVITY	MONDAY	TUESDAY	WEDNESDAY	THURSDAY	FRIDAY
1st PERIOD	☒	☒	■	☒	□
2nd PERIOD	■	☒	☒	■	■
3rd PERIOD	☑	■	☑	☑	☑
4th PERIOD	■	☑	☑	☑	☑
5th PERIOD	☑	■	☑	☑	☑
6th PERIOD	☑	■	■	■	■
7th PERIOD	☑	☑	☑	☑	☑
8th PERIOD	■	☑	■	☑	■

COLLECTING BASELINE DATA

Just as you would with your students, it is important to know your current rate of OTR to effectively develop a plan to increase it. To start, you will use the instructional time you previously identified to determine a specific time to collect the data. The time you select should be when you are delivering instruction and not during other activities such as independent work time. Although you can collect data throughout the entire lesson, you can also just focus on a smaller amount of time. For example, a ninth-grade biology teacher may have instruction during the first 30 minutes of the period but may only collect data on the first 10 minutes.

Next, you will want to identify the data you want to collect and determine how you will collect the data. This can be done in a variety of ways and will most likely depend on the resources available to you. The first option is to collect data on your own behavior while you are teaching. If choosing this option, it may be best to simply tally the overall frequency of OTRs. This can be done by making tally marks on a clipboard or using a handheld tally counter and then transferring it to a more formal data collection form like the one seen in Figure 3. While this option requires very few resources, it also has its drawbacks. First, it can be difficult to accurately collect data on your own behavior in real time, and second, you are limited to only collecting overall OTR frequency.

FIGURE 3 ● Sample OTR data collection form

DATE	TIME	OTR TOTAL	OTR RATE
Dates: 10/22–11/19		**Classroom/class period observed:** 1st period	
Name: Donita Varmitek			
10/22	9:00–9:20	9	0.45 per min.
10/27	9:00–9:20	12	0.60 per min.
11/5	9:00–9:20	20	1.00 per min.
11/12	9:00–9:20	10	0.50 per min.
11/19	9:00–9:20	18	0.90 per min.
Average		13.8	0.69 per min.

Note: OTR, opportunity to respond.

Because it may be difficult to collect data on your own behavior while simultaneously trying to teach, there are a few other options you can choose. First, you can ask a colleague (e.g., teacher, paraprofessional, counselor, assistant principal,

principal) in the building to observe you. Although this is the most efficient way to collect the data, a colleague may not be available during your identified time. In that case you may consider video recording the session and collecting the data at a later time. Although both of these approaches require extra resources and/or time, they allow you to collect data more accurately and in greater detail. For example, Figure 4 shows a data collection sheet that differentiates OTR from individual OTR and group OTR, as well as the specific strategies described in this book.

FIGURE 4 ● Sample OTR data collection differentiating group and individual strategies

Date: 2/2		**Classroom/class period observed:** Mathematics
Length of observation: 20 Minutes		
Observer: Malik Alexander		

OTR INDIVIDUAL	**OTR GROUP**	**OTR TOTAL**
卌 IIII	IIII	13

Which OTR were used? (check all that apply)	☐ Whip around	☐ Quick poll	☒ Choral responding
	☐ Stop and jot	☐ Guided notes	☐ Response cards
	☐ Hand signals	☒ Turn and talk	☐ Cued retell
	☐ Four corners	☐ Snowball	☐ Classroom mingle
	☒ Individual	☐ Response slates	☐ Numbered heads together

Note: OTR, opportunity to respond.

INCORPORATE OTR INTO LESSON PLANNING

Providing OTRs at sufficient rates may not come naturally to some. For this reason it will be helpful to purposefully incorporate OTRs into your lesson planning. Although you might choose only one OTR strategy to master in the beginning, using a variety of OTRs is recommended to promote mixed responding (i.e., individually and in unison). Research suggests that mixed responding is most effective when it is delivered at a ratio of 70% responding in unison and 30% individual responding (Haydon, Conroy et al., 2010; Haydon et al., 2013). When selecting OTR strategies, it is important to consider the context of the lesson or activity, the students' characteristics and needs, access to resources, and efficiency of implementation.

CONTEXT OF THE LESSON/ACTIVITY

Each strategy in this book is most effective when used in the proper context of the lesson. For example, if the purpose of the activity is to do a brief review of previously learned content before moving on to new content, you may choose strategies such as response cards, hand signals, choral responding, and classroom mingle. On the other hand, if your intent is to have a more in-depth discussion on a topic, you would maybe choose strategies such as turn and talk, four corners, and snowball.

STUDENT CHARACTERISTICS AND NEEDS

It is important to keep your students' characteristics and needs in mind, both as a whole class and as individuals, when selecting strategies for your lesson. This will include considering skills related to academic proficiency as well as classroom management. For example, guided notes are generally used in grades 3 through 12 because younger students are not as proficient in writing. If you were to use this strategy with younger students, you would need to make sure that their responses are very brief (i.e., one word). Similarly, a strategy such as cued retell will not be effective if the students are not able to read the cue sheet. Knowing your students' ability to follow multistep directions is important because it allows you to determine if a visual or anchor chart will support the students or a different strategy is needed. Additionally, some strategies such as four corners and snowball require efficient and effective transitions. Knowing this can allow you to determine if verbal reminders and timers can help with transitioning or a different strategy is needed.

Keeping in mind individual student characteristics and needs when selecting strategies is critical when planning your lesson. Although a strategy may be effective as is for most students, differentiation will need to occur for others to be successful. Although this book addresses some possible ways to differentiate for diverse learners, it cannot possibly address them all. You as the teacher will best know your students and what they will need to be successful. For example, when planning for the use of the whip around strategy, you may strategically order your students so that you call on a particular impulsive student first so that he or she does not try to yell while others are sharing.

ACCESS TO RESOURCES

The strategy you use will be dependent on the resources available to you and your students. If not already available, you may need to prepare the materials required to implement the strategy. Once created, some materials can be used and reused without modification. For example, response cards and response slates can be used repeatedly. Other materials, such as guided notes and cued retell sheets, will need to be adapted to the content of the upcoming lesson. Considering access to resources is also important in the virtual environment. For example, if a teacher is planning to use response cards or response slates for online instruction, they will need to make sure that all students have the necessary materials beforehand and are reminded to bring them to the class session.

EFFICIENCY OF IMPLEMENTATION

Efficiently implementing the strategy is important to its effectiveness. For this reason you may want to preplan the questions or prompts that will align with the strategy you have chosen. For example, when planning to use response cards to review identifying subject and verb, the teacher would identify a range of examples of both a subject and a verb. This would include words related to people, places, things, qualities, and ideas (i.e., subjects) as well as words related to mind or body actions (i.e., verbs). Without preplanning, the teacher may not give the full range of examples needed to effectively review the content.

Preplanning the questions and prompts also allows the teacher to identify follow-up questions for specific individuals to differentiate instruction. When using response cards to review subject and verb, the teacher can identify specific students to ask why they think the word is a subject or a verb. The teacher can also identify some students to ask if they agree or disagree with the other student's answer. Preplanning who will receive certain follow-up questions decreases the chances that a student may feel embarrassed by not knowing an answer.

Efficient implementation is also dependent on how well a teacher manages time. As you have probably noticed, all of these strategies have a suggested amount of time to be effective. The teacher will need to preplan the amount of time that will be sufficient for their students and have a method of recording this time (e.g., with a digital timer, visual timer, watch, or smartphone). It should be noted that although you preplan the amount of time, it can always be adjusted during the activity if you notice that students may need more or less time.

Along with selecting the OTR strategy, efficient implementation will be dependent on how fluent the students are with the response routine. As discussed in the Introduction, teachers should identify a response routine that best fits their teaching style and the students' preference. But no matter what the selected response routine or OTR strategy is, the routine will need to be explicitly taught to the students and used consistently to be effective. To explicitly teach the response routine, the teacher can first model the strategy and routine for the students. This will be followed by having them practice the routine with an easier and/or higher-interest topic. As the students begin to learn the response routine, the teacher can gradually fade the support by creating visual aids as a reminder for them.

GOAL SETTING AND FEEDBACK

As a teacher you are regularly setting goals for students as a means to determine success or failure on a skill, concept, or standard. And although you may have long-term goals for students to achieve by the end of the year, you would never expect student mastery on these goals at the beginning of the year. Instead, you create several short-term goals that will maintain sufficient progress toward meeting those long-term goals. Likewise, setting short-term goals for your performance to achieve a long-term goal will be important for your success. For example, as previously discussed, it is well accepted that using a range of OTRs during instruction at rates at or above three per minute is associated with positive student outcomes (Haydon et al., 2010; Sutherland et al., 2003). However, a teacher may collect baseline data and discover that they are

TABLE 2 ● Delivery of feedback

LEVEL OF INTENSITY	DELIVERY OF FEEDBACK	TYPE OF FEEDBACK	EXAMPLE
LEAST (top) ... MOST (bottom)	End of day/week/month	Verbal	Verbal feedback delivered at the end of the day or week on the frequency or rate of OTRs. Feedback can include a brief anecdotal summary of observation.
		Written	Written feedback delivered at the end of the day or week on the frequency or rate of OTRs. Feedback can include a brief anecdotal narrative of observation and be delivered via handwritten note or email.
	End of lesson	Visual	Visual feedback delivered graphically on the frequency or rate of OTRs. Graph includes outcomes from previous observations.
		Verbal	Verbal feedback delivered immediately following the lesson or class period on the frequency or rate of OTRs.
		Written	Written feedback delivered immediately following the lesson or class period on the frequency or rate of OTRs. Feedback can include a brief anecdotal narrative of observation and be delivered via a handwritten note.
	During lesson	Verbal	Verbal feedback prompting the teacher to give students OTR by using bug-in-ear technology (e.g., wireless headphones and microphone).
		Visual	Visual feedback prompting the teacher to give OTR to students by using response cards (e.g., index card labeled "OTR").

Note: OTR, opportunity to respond.

providing OTRs at a rate well below one per minute. Providing three OTRs per minute would be an unrealistic expectation to achieve in a day, week, or month and could possibly set this teacher up for failure. It may be more appropriate to set three OTRs as a long-term objective, with several short-term goals that would gradually lead up to the desired criterion.

One way to help achieve your goals is to ask another teacher to assist with goal setting and monitoring through peer coaching. Peer coaching is where teachers observe each other and provide support, feedback, and assistance in a none-valuative manner (Ackland, 1991; Valencia & Killion, 1988). The peer coaching model has been shown to be effective in increasing teachers' use of instructional practices and behavioral strategies (Bethune & Wood, 2013; Cornelius et al., 2019; Kretlow & Bartholomew, 2010). As shown in Table 2, there are many ways you can receive feedback that ranges in intensity, including after the lesson and during the lesson.

COLLECTING AND ANALYZING DATA

Regardless of the type of delivery you choose, there are additional things you may want to consider. First, you may want to determine how often to collect data. Ideally, you would want to collect data frequently (e.g., daily, biweekly), especially when first starting. Then, you could gradually decrease the frequency (e.g., weekly, bimonthly, monthly) as you become more comfortable with your delivery of OTR. In reality, it will most likely be dependent on who is collecting the data. For example, it may not be feasible to collect data on yourself frequently. And if you are having colleagues observe, they may not be available as often as you would prefer. If you are not able to collect data as frequently as you would like, that is okay. The goal should be to monitor in the most efficient and practical way so that you continue monitoring your progress.

Along with determining when to collect data and goal setting, it is important to consider how to collect and organize data. It can be rather difficult to see patterns in your progress when looking at a long list of numbers or separate data collection sheets. Graphs can provide a visual aide to help evaluate your progress in an effective and efficient manner. There are several different types of graphs that can help you analyze data, including bar graphs, circle graphs, and line graphs, all of which can be easily created by hand with graphing paper or electronically. Choosing the right graph(s) will depend on what data you want to analyze.

A circle graph, or pie chart, can be useful because it will show how the whole is broken down into related parts. The circle graph can then represent either frequencies or percentages of the whole. Figure 5 provides examples of how pie graphs can be used to analyze OTRs. The circle graph on the left shows how you can differentiate between group OTRs and individual OTRs. This can be useful for a teacher attempting to provide the ratio of 70% responding in unison and 30% individual responding that Haydon and colleagues (Haydon, Conroy, et al., 2010; Haydon et al., 2013) have recommended. On the other hand, the circle graph on the right shows an example of differentiating between the various strategies of OTR used in a lesson. This can be helpful for a teacher who is interested in providing a mixture of OTR strategies in each lesson.

Another graph that can be useful in analyzing data is the bar graph. It can represent frequencies, rate, or percentages. Like the circle graph the bar graph can compare items. For example, Figure 6 provides examples of how bar graphs can be used to analyze OTRs. The top bar graph compares overall rate of OTRs, group OTRs, and individual OTRs, while the bottom bar graph shows the frequencies of strategies used over a period of a month. Unlike the circle graph the bar graph can also show change over time.

The line graph may be the most effective for showing a visual pattern of changes over time. Showing individual data points that are connected by a line allows you to evaluate the direction or trend of your performance and judge it against a criterion. Elements of a line graph that can help with analyzing the data collected include aim lines and trend lines.

FIGURE 5 ● OTR pie graphs

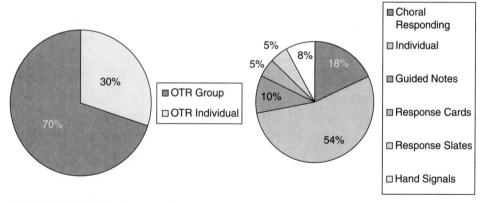

Note: OTR, opportunity to respond.

FIGURE 6 ● OTR bar graphs

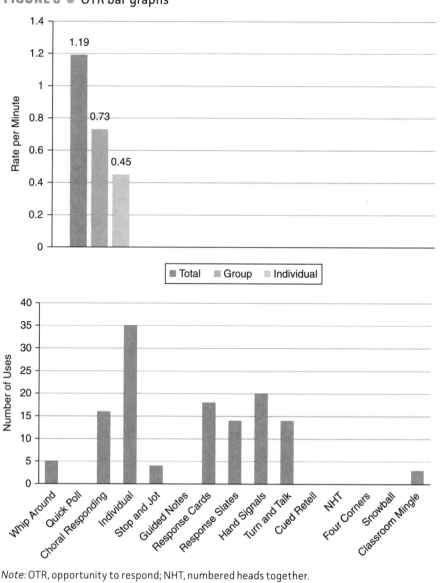

Note: OTR, opportunity to respond; NHT, numbered heads together.

AIM LINES

An aim line will connect the current level of performance (i.e., baseline data) to a criterion level of performance at some point in the future. For example, a teacher's baseline data may indicate that they are currently providing OTRs at a rate of 1 per minute, and they then decide to set a goal that they will provide an average of 1.5 OTRs per minute in 20 school days. In this case the teacher would draw a line from the median baseline data point to a point designating the desired rate and date. Aim lines represent the minimal line of progress, which helps with analyzing your performance. You will know that you are making adequate progress toward your goal as long as your performance is at or above your aim line. On the other hand, if your performance is below the aim line, you may need to make some changes. A general rule of thumb is that your performance is still adequate if the data do not fall below the aim line for more than two consecutive days. However, three consecutive data points below the aim line indicates inadequate progress.

TREND LINES

A trend line, also called a line of best fit, is a line plotted through a set of existing data points that will help predict the general direction of your performance. When paired with an aim line, the trend line will allow you to predict if you are going to meet your goal by the date you selected. Trend lines can be produced pretty easily on electronic spreadsheets or created by hand with graphing paper. To calculate by hand, you will need to have a minimum of six data points and know how to calculate the median rate (midrate) and date (middate). The midrate is the median data point running up the ordinate, or y-axis, and the mid-date is the median data point running across the abscissa, or x-axis. From there, you will simply calculate the mid-rate and mid-date intersections of the first and last three data points and draw a line connecting the two intersections.

CONCLUDING THOUGHTS

Providing a range of OTRs at sufficient rates may at first seem like an overwhelming task, especially with all of the other responsibilities a teacher may have. But our hope is that the suggestions provided in this section will support you in this endeavor. Although it may initially take a little more time to prepare lessons and more intensive feedback may be needed to be successful, the provision of OTRs will become more second nature with repeated use, feedback, and experience. The process will simply become part of your natural teaching.

Appendix A

STOP-AND-JOT TEMPLATE
ELEMENTARY

Name _____   Week_____

1 STOP	
2 STOP	
3 STOP	
4 STOP	
5 STOP	

Image source: pixabay.com/OpenIcons

online resources 🔖 Available for download at **resources.corwin.com/CreatingAnActivelyEngagedClassroom**

Appendix B

STOP-AND-JOT TEMPLATE
SECONDARY

Name _____   Date_____

Read the following questions below. Be prepared to jot down your thoughts when prompted.

QUESTION:

QUESTION:

QUESTION:

Appendix C

RESPONSE CARD TEMPLATES

Yes	**No**
True	**False**
Agree 👍	**Disagree** 👎

Image source: pixabay.com/OpenClipart-Vectors

Available for download at **resources.corwin.com/CreatingAnActivelyEngagedClassroom**

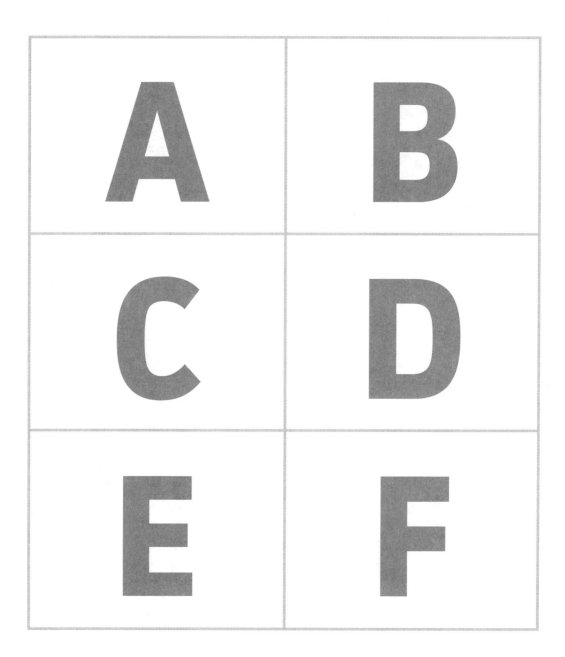

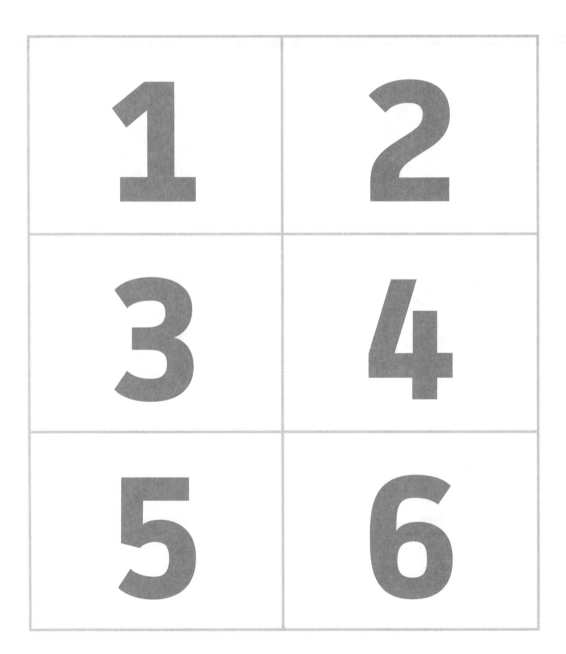

Appendix D

FIST-TO-FIVE VISUAL

Image source: pixabay.com/OpenClipart-Vectors

Appendix E

THUMBS UP/THUMBS DOWN VISUAL

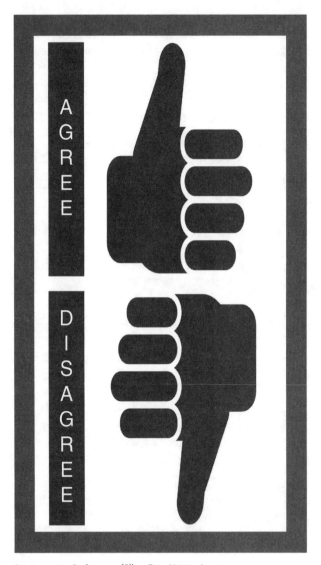

Image source: pixabay.com/Clker-Free-Vector-Images

online resources ☞ Available for download at **resources.corwin.com/CreatingAnActivelyEngagedClassroom**

Appendix F

THUMBS UP/THUMBS DOWN/ THUMBS SIDEWAYS VISUAL

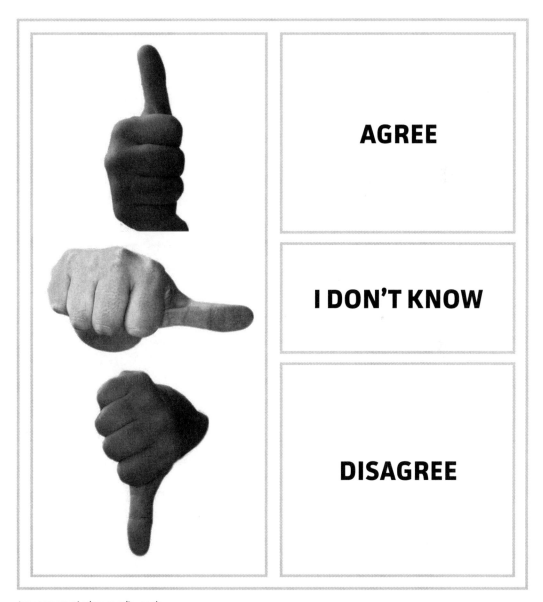

Image source: pixabay.com/jc_cards

Appendix G

CUED-RETELL SHEET

Name _____   Date_____

Partner's Name _____

Put a check under the "Independent" column as your partner recalls items below. If your partner does not remember an item, offer cues to assist with recalling the information and put a check under the "Cues" column.

CONCEPTS/TERMS	INDEPENDENT	CUES
1.		
2.		
3.		
4.		
5.		
6.		
7.		
8.		
9.		
10.		

online resources 🏹 Available for download at **resources.corwin.com/CreatingAnActivelyEngagedClassroom**

Appendix H

OTR DATA COLLECTION FORM

OVERALL OTR ONLY

Dates: ___/___/___ - ___/___/___   Classroom/class period observed: _____

Name: _____

DATE	TIME	OTR TOTAL	OTR PER MIN.
AVERAGE			

Appendix I

OTR DATA COLLECTION FORM

INDIVIDUAL/GROUP OTR–SPECIFIC STRATEGIES USED

Date: _____   Classroom/class period observed: _____

Length of observation: _____   Observer: _____

Directions: Tally number of occurrences

OTR INDIVIDUAL	OTR GROUP	OTR TOTAL	OTR PER MINUTE

Which OTR were used?

(check all that apply)

☐ Whip around   ☐ Quick poll   ☐ Choral responding   ☐ Individual

☐ Stop and jot   ☐ Guided notes   ☐ Response cards   ☐ Response slates

☐ Hand signals   ☐ Turn and talk   ☐ Cued retell   ☐ Numbered heads together

☐ Four corners   ☐ Snowball   ☐ Classroom mingle

online resources 🔍 Available for download at **resources.corwin.com/CreatingAnActivelyEngagedClassroom**

References

Ackland, R. (1991). A review of the peer coaching literature. *Journal of Staff Development,* 1(12), 22–27.

Archer, A. L., & Hughes, C. A. (2011). *Explicit instruction: Effective and efficient teaching.* Guilford Press.

Bethune, K. S., & Wood, C. L. (2013). Effects of coaching on teachers' use of function-based interventions for students with severe disabilities. *Teacher Education and Special Education,* 36(2), 97–114. https://doi.org/10.1177/0888406413478637

Brophy, J., & Good, T. (1986). Teacher behavior and student achievement. In M. C. Wittrock (Ed.), *Handbook of research on teaching* (3rd ed., pp. 328–375). Macmillan.

Chetty, R., Friedman, J. N., & Rockoff, J. E. (2011). *The long-term impacts of teachers: Teacher value-added and student outcomes in adulthood* (No. w17699). National Bureau of Economic Research. https://doi.org/10.3386/w17699

Christenson, S. L., Reschly, A. L., & Wylie, C. (Eds.). (2012). *Handbook of research on student engagement.* Springer Science & Business Media. https://doi.org/10.1007/978–1–4614–2018–7

Cornelius, K. E., Rosenberg, M. S., & Sandmel, K. N. (2019). Examining the impact of professional development and coaching on mentoring of novice special educators. *Action in Teacher Education,* 42(3), 253–270. https://doi.org/10.1080/01626620.2019.1638847

Gage, N., Scott, T. M., Hirn, R. G., & MacSuga-Gage, A. (2018). The relationship between teachers' implementation of classroom management practices and student behavior in elementary school. *Behavioral Disorders,* 43(2), 302–315. https://doi.org/10.1177/0198742917714809

Hattie, J. A. C. (2009). *Visible learning: A synthesis of over 800 meta-analyses relating to achievement.* Routledge.

Haydon, T., Conroy, M., Scott, T. M., Sindelar, P., Barber, B. R., & Orlando, A. (2010). A comparison of three types of opportunities to respond on student academic and social behaviors. *Journal of Emotional and Behavioral Disorders,* 18(1), 27–40. https://doi.org/10.1177/1063426609333448

Haydon, T., Maheady, L., & Hunter, W. (2010). Effects of numbered heads together on the daily quiz scores and on-task behavior of students with disabilities. *Journal of Behavioral Education,* 19(3), 222–238. https://doi.org/10.1007/s10864–010–9108–3

Haydon, T., Marsicano, R., & Scott, T. M. (2013). A comparison of choral and individual responding: A review of the literature. *Preventing School Failure: Alternative Education for Children and Youth,* 57(4), 181–188. https://doi.org/10.1080/1045988X.2012.682184

Hunter, W., & Haydon, T. (2013). Examining the effectiveness of numbered heads together for students with emotional and behavioral disorders. *Beyond Behavior,* 22(3), 40–45. https://doi.org/10.1177/107429561302200306

Kagan, S. (1992). *Cooperative learning* (7th ed.). Resources for Teachers.

King, M. L., Jr. (1947). The purpose of education. *The Maroon Tiger,* 10, 123–124.

Kretlow, A. G., & Bartholomew, C. C. (2010). Using coaching to improve the fidelity of evidence-based practices: A review of studies. *Teacher Education and Special Education,* 33(4), 279–299. https://doi.org/10.1177/0888406410371643

Maheady, L., Mallette, B., Harper, G., & Sacca, K. (1991). Numbered heads together: A peer-mediated option for improving the academic achievement of heterogeneous learning groups. *Remedial and Special Education*, 12(2), 25–33. https://doi.org/10.1177/074193259101200206

Maheady, L., Michielli-Pendl, J., Harper, G., & Mallette, B. (2006). The effects of numbered heads together with and without an incentive package on the science test performance of a diverse group of sixth graders. *Journal of Behavioral Education*, 15, 25–39. https://doi.org/10.1007/s10864-005-9002-6

McLeskey, J., Barringer, M.-D., Billingsley, B., Brownell, M., Jackson, D., Kennedy, M., Lewis, T., Maheady, L., Rodriquez, J., Scheeler, M. C., Winn, J., & Ziegler, D. (2017). *High-leverage practices in special education*. Council for Exceptional Children; CEEDAR Center.

Reschly, A. L., & Christenson, S. L. (2006). Prediction of dropout among students with mild disabilities: A case for the inclusion of student engagement variables. *Remedial and Special Education*, 27(5), 276–292. https://doi.org/10.1177/07419325060270050301

Scott, T. M., & Gage, N. (2020). An examination of the association between teacher's instructional practices and school-wide disciplinary and academic outcomes. *Education and Treatment of Children*. https://www.x-mol.com/paperRedirect/1288888888940216320

Scott, T. M., Hirn, R. G., & Cooper, J. T. (2017). *Teacher and student behaviors: Keys to success in classroom instruction*. Rowan & Littlefield.

Stockard, J. Wood, T. W., Coughlin, C., & Khoury, C. R. (2018). The effectiveness of direct instruction curricula: A meta-analysis of a half century of research. *Review of Educational Research*, 88(4), 479–507. https://doi.org/10.3102/0034654317751919

Stronge, J. (2013). *Effective teachers = student achievement: What the research says*. Routledge. https://doi.org/10.4324/9781315854977

Sutherland, K. S., Adler, N., & Gunter, P. L. (2003). The effects of varying rates of opportunities to respond to academic requests on the classroom behavior of students with EBD. *Journal of Emotional and Behavioral Disorders*, 11, 239–248. https://doi.org/10.1177/10634266030110040501

Teasley, A. B. (1996). New teachers: Dealing effectively with student behavior. *English Journal*, 85(4), 80–81. https://doi.org/10.2307/819649

Touchette, P. E., MacDonald, R. F., & Langer, S. N. (1985). A scatter plot for identifying stimulus control of problem behavior. *Journal of Applied Behavior Analysis*, 18(4), 343–351. https://doi.org/10.1901/jaba.1985.18-343

Valencia, S. W., & Killion, J. P. (1988). Overcoming obstacles to teacher change: Direction from school-based efforts. *Journal of Staff Development*, 9(2), 2–8.

Index